אֵיכָה *Ayeka*

THE AYEKA HAGGADAH

This haggadah is dedicated to my *bashert*, Sara Yehudit.

"Exodus" is the personal journey to freedom that waits for every one of us. Long ago, the Jewish People traveled together. It is too daunting to journey alone.

Sara Yehudit, you have been God's loving messenger and co-sojourner in my life. I did not and could not begin my journey until I met you. You created space for me to hear the prayer of my soul and find the courage to take my first steps. You are the one who enables me and so many others to hear our own voice.

The *Ayeka* Haggadah
Hearing Your Own Voice: A Guide for All Ages to Personalize Your Seder
2017 Quality Paperback Edition, First Printing
© 2017 by Aryeh Ben David

ISBN: 978-0-692-83289-9

Design: Jen Klor, Jerusalem
Cover art: *Bereshit* by Yoram Raanan

Ayeka LTD
c/o Nina Bruder
3616 Henry Hudson Pkwy Apt. 2BS
Bronx, NY 10463

The Ayeka Haggadah

HEARING YOUR OWN VOICE

A guide for all ages to personalize your seder

ARYEH BEN DAVID

Contents

Introduction

"Where am I this Passover? Where are we?"

The goal of this haggadah is to make it easy—or at least easier—to run a personal and meaningful Seder.

The idea for the project came to me after one particular Passover Seder when we had a challenging mix of guests of various backgrounds and ages around the table. As I prepared for the evening, I found myself panicking:

○ Will they be bored? How can I make it interesting, exciting?

○ Everyone is at such different levels of understanding and interest. How can I engage the kids and, at the same time, the parents, cousins, friends, and students?

○ **How is it possible to make the night meaningful, memorable, and impactful for me and these wonderful people?**

As usual, I bought a new haggadah, searching for insights that would capture everyone's interest and keep us all engaged. I quoted wise rabbis and scholars, experimented with tricks and games, all trying to "give over" the experience of leaving Egypt.

The Seder went well. People were happy with it. But for me, two unsettling questions remained:

1. Did we really focus—together—on the primary theme of Passover? People participated but, overall, the conversation seemed disjointed. The comments, questions, and insights did not seem to build on each other in a coherent way.

2. Was the Seder personal enough? Did we have a meaningful experience? Did the Seder affect and impact the lives of those at our table?

Despite being "pretty good," it was clear to me that the Seder experience at our table was just not good enough, not what I wanted it to be.

Thinking it through afterward, it was easy for me to see why. We had learned the haggadah and talked about leaving Egypt, but we had not made it personal. Each of us—whether we are eight, eighteen, or seventy-eight—is living a personal journey, and the haggadah is the paradigm of all journeys. If we stop leading or teaching others, and begin opening and inviting others, then our guests will actually be able to discover and share how the Exodus experience is affecting them now. The haggadah has the potential to be a personal and intimate guide to transform this night of nights for individuals, families, and communities.

The goal of this haggadah is to help you change the tone and direction around your Seder table—to transform "The Story" into "My Story." It encourages you and your Seder guests to ask: "How is my journey going? How am I traveling as an individual, as a part of our family, as a part of my community, and as part of the Jewish People?"

This shift is actually easy to achieve, because you just open up the Seder to everyone present.

The evocative, associative material is already present in the text of the haggadah. The purpose of this haggadah is to create a framework of questions, to gently invite and direct everyone to move the story *inward*, to help them see the journey of the Jews as their own journey. We are engaging in an eternal story. What better time to re-experience and share our personal challenges than when we imagine standing up to Pharaoh, withstanding the plagues, and crossing the Red Sea?

Once we approach the haggadah with this mind-set, the Seder stops being a ritual or a performance and starts becoming a personal experience. As we connect our own journeys with those who came before us, we also connect more closely with each other. We are all kindred spirits on this journey.

The key is set out in the structure of the haggadah itself: the questions, food, and drama. Even one key question—if it is the right question—can be enough for the whole evening:

o   "We are here, together, reading these words, reliving this journey. What does 'leaving Egypt' evoke for me right now? What does it mean for us, for our People?"

o   "What is my Promised Land? Where are we headed?"

o   "What is holding me back from journeying?"

The goal of this haggadah, then, is to encourage each person at your Seder table to say to themselves: **The Seder is about figuring out where I fit in, right now, in the development of my own life, the life of my family, and the life of my People.**

In truth, almost none of the Jews who left Egypt actually entered the Promised Land. They wandered for forty years in the wilderness. Paradise is elusive, and its pursuit is challenging. While moving forward, we often stumble, wander aimlessly, run in circles. **For two thousand years, the haggadah has been the Jewish People's invitation to ask: "Where are we now on the journey?" When you encourage each person to give voice to the personal, the haggadah can perform magic.**

Give it a try. I hope that the questions and activities you encounter in this haggadah will help you find your way.

How to Use This Haggadah

If we want the Passover Seder to be personal, meaningful, and memorable, we have to begin with some thoughtful preparation. There is just no other way.

I promise that this is easier than it sounds. In fact, it is a lot easier than running a Seder the "normal" way. With a little investment of thought and preparation—by thinking through the questions posed in this haggadah prior to the Seder and asking your guests to do the same—you can place yourself and your guests emotionally, personally, and spiritually at the starting point for the journey of journeys, ready to hit the ground running when you pour that first glass of wine.

Very Important: One Hour of Prep Time, *Before* the Seder

The best way to use this haggadah is to invite everyone to read it and respond to the writing exercises ahead of time, preferably during the week *before* the Seder itself. Preparation for each participant should take less than one hour.

Don't wait for the Seder! Like all key moments in our lives, we need to prepare.

The Questions

In this haggadah, we offer forty different questions, that is, forty different opportunities for engaging personally with the haggadah. You don't have to answer them all, just the ones that personally speak to you. The questions and activites are color-coded into five different tracks, and hopefully many will appeal to you and your guests.

Ten questions for kids: They deal primarily with the first sections of the haggadah, with the goal of engaging kids before they disengage—or fall asleep!

Ten questions for everyone, designed to elicit short answers: These ten questions open the floor for everyone to share something personal but only require short answers. They bring guests into the Seder without making "too big a deal of it."

Three questions for everyone, designed to elicit longer, more thoughtful responses. These sections are specially designed as conversations for pairs (*chevruta*). These three questions invite a deeper and more personal conversation. To include everyone, we suggest a bit of stage management: ask everyone to turn to the person next to them and talk for a few minutes about what they wrote and what this question brings up for them. This mini-*chevruta* allows for more privacy and shakes up the group-reading dynamic. Allow two to three minutes for the first partner, and then switch. Conclude by asking if anyone would like to share with the group.

Fifteen sections for everyone—the "Hope-Giver" ideas: Explained in the next chapter, page 12.

Two questions for seniors: Our elders have so much wisdom and experience to offer, yet they often feel left out. These two opportunities offer them center stage, giving them a chance to share their stories with the next generation.

The Plan

Give a copy of this haggadah to each of your guests. Ask them to read it through and answer the questions in writing. Encourage guests with small children to work through the haggadah together. **Write in the haggadah itself!** Each piece has sections for personal writing, with an extra writing page at the back for those who need more space.

This pre-Seder preparation will take less than one hour. It offers time for reflection, for a check-in that gets everyone into the Seder frame of mind. **This one hour can make the difference between a Seder that is just like last year's and a Seder that will be different from all other nights.**

At the Seder

When guests have already prepared, your role as leader becomes incredibly simple.

All you have to do is read a section of the haggadah—or invite someone else to read a section—and then ask everyone, "Who would 11 like to share their response to this question? Who would like to begin our conversation?"

The pressure is off. You don't have to illuminate or entertain. Your job is to create the space for everyone to feel comfortable, to participate, and to share. The floor is open—everyone will want to hear what others have to say, and many will want to share.

With forty different questions—forty opportunities to share—there is more than enough material to fill the evening. I actually do not suggest covering all forty questions unless you want to sit at the Seder table until sunrise, like the haggadah's famous rabbis. In fact, the biggest challenge for the Seder leader will be to keep from getting stuck too long on one question!

The Hope-Giver Theme

The Exodus has given hope to generations—and this year, at our Seder, we need to give hope to ourselves.

Over three thousand years ago, a group of people, enslaved for generations, lost hope of ever being free. No slave had ever escaped from Egypt, and the Jewish slaves had given up calling out for help. When Moses promised them freedom, they couldn't even listen. Yet, just one year later, this powerless group had awakened, challenged the world's strongest leader, and emerged triumphant.

This outlandishly radical, impossible story of success is a paradigm of hope that has inspired people of all faiths and nationalities throughout the centuries.

Hope is the most precious gift that exists. The mystics would say that our soul is hardwired for hope. We surely feel better about ourselves and others when hope fills our being. Yet hope withers easily in the face of disappointment and hardship. We are afraid that our dreams will lead to disappointment, and it is all too easy to become disillusioned toxic cynics who ridicule optimists and visionaries. The hopeless state drains the light of our eyes and the health of our bodies.

Then comes the Passover Seder, the antidote to hopelessness. The Exodus story is an overcoming of impossible odds, a triumph over all-powerful enemies. Reliving the Exodus gives us the will and strength to hope once again, to rediscover our vision of a better world, and a better "me."

Hope is the gift the Jews have given to the world, and hope is the most important gift we can give each other during our Seder. By reliving the haggadah, we refill our hope-tanks with strong fuel from the deepest reservoirs.

To begin the refueling, we have designated fifteen questions as Hope-Givers. Each one gives us the opportunity to let go of our disappointments and to discover the resolve we need to take our next positive steps.

Though we are no longer slaves, we each remain stuck in some part of our lives. The Passover Seder is a de-stuckifying experience.

This is not always easy. Getting unstuck—making changes—is scary and can overwhelm us. It makes us venture into the unknown and take risks. We may fail; we may wander for years in the desert. Toddlers don't begin walking without falling hard and often. But they don't stay down; they get up and move forward.

Hope is the springboard for our next steps. We need to replenish our personal hope-tanks, to bond with kindred supportive spirits, to embrace the challenge of changing ourselves and the world. Hope has been the soul of the Jewish People for over three thousand years. Moses said to Pharaoh, "Let my People go!" We have to ingest these words anew every year, in order to strengthen ourselves and to overcome the fear of the unknown, to march forward, slowly but defiantly, toward the Promised Land.

THE HAGGADAH: Pre-Seder Check-in

(Write your answers in the circles.)

Where are you (*ayeka*) regarding the Passover Seder this year?

What are you excited about for this Seder?

What would you hope to happen for yourself and others at the Seder?

If you were to
design a t-shirt that
perfectly describes
your Seder, what
would it look like?

kids

hope-giver

Beautiful Passover Dishes

Suffering makes us question the presence of God in this world, the scope of our control, and the hope of a better future. To the extent that we feel guilty and blame ourselves for bringing about our own suffering, we may lose hope in ourselves.

The Jews' prolonged suffering in Egypt made them unable to hear Moses' inspiring words or to imagine a brighter future. Their lives had been utterly darkened.

In the beginning of Genesis, we read about the flood and the destruction of the world. After forty days of rain, Noah emerges from the ark to encounter a world of death and desolation. Everything has been destroyed. How can he possibly go on? What purpose is there in rebuilding?

God gives Noah the antidote to despair—the rainbow. God could have simply said, "I will never destroy the world again." But God does more than that. He shows Noah the rainbow.

The rainbow is the epitome of all beauty. It encompasses all colors, all wavelengths. **Within the rainbow is concealed all possibilities of future beauty.**

After destruction and suffering, beauty gives us hope.

Some people save their most beautiful dishes to use just one night a year at the Passover Seder. What one item of special beauty would you want to add to your Seder table this year?

15

THE SEDER

THE SEDER PLATE

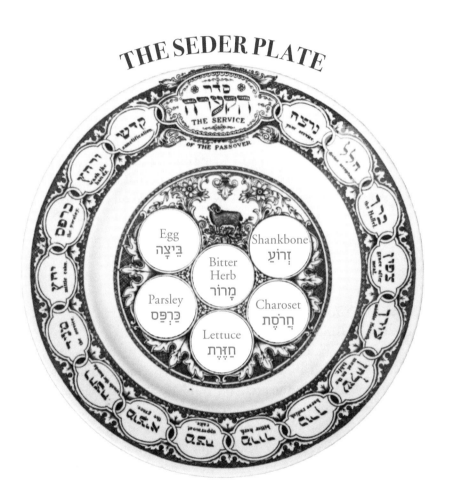

Kadesh ◦ קַדֵּשׁ ◦ Kiddush

Urchatz ◦ וּרְחַץ ◦ Washing Hands

Karpas ◦ כַּרְפַּס ◦ Vegetable

Yachatz ◦ יַחַץ ◦ Breaking the Middle Matzah

Maggid ◦ מַגִּיד ◦ Retelling the Passover Story

Rachtzah ◦ רָחְצָה ◦ Washing Hands

Motzi Matzah ◦ מוֹצִיא מַצָּה ◦ Eating Matzah

Maror ◦ מָרוֹר ◦ The Bitter Herb

Korech ◦ כּוֹרֵךְ ◦ Mixing Bitter and Sweet

Shulchan Orech ◦ שֻׁלְחָן עוֹרֵךְ ◦ Let's Eat

Tzafun ◦ צָפוּן ◦ Afikoman

Barech ◦ בָּרֵךְ ◦ Blessing the Meal

Hallel ◦ הַלֵּל ◦ Praising God

Nirtzah ◦ נִרְצָה ◦ Closing

Kadesh ∘ קַדֵּשׁ ∘ Kiddush

First Cup of Wine

We pour the first cup. The matzot are uncovered. On Shabbat, begin here:

הִנְנִי מוּכָן וּמְזֻמָּן לְקַיֵּם מִצְוַת כּוֹס רִאשׁוֹן מֵאַרְבַּע כּוֹסוֹת
לְשֵׁם יְחוּד קוּדְשָׁא בְּרִיךְ הוּא וּשְׁכִינְתֵּיהּ עַל יְדֵי הַהוּא טָמִיר
וְנֶעְלָם בְּשֵׁם כָּל־יִשְׂרָאֵל.

I am ready and willing to enact the precept of blessing this day over the first cup of wine. I do this to unite God's Presence and in the name of all of Israel.

וַיְהִי עֶרֶב וַיְהִי בֹקֶר יוֹם הַשִּׁשִּׁי, וַיְכֻלּוּ הַשָּׁמַיִם וְהָאָרֶץ וְכָל־צְבָאָם.
וַיְכַל אֱלֹהִים בַּיּוֹם הַשְּׁבִיעִי, מְלַאכְתּוֹ אֲשֶׁר עָשָׂה, וַיִּשְׁבֹּת
בַּיּוֹם הַשְּׁבִיעִי, מִכָּל־מְלַאכְתּוֹ אֲשֶׁר עָשָׂה. וַיְבָרֶךְ אֱלֹהִים אֶת־
יוֹם הַשְּׁבִיעִי, וַיְקַדֵּשׁ אֹתוֹ, כִּי בוֹ שָׁבַת מִכָּל־מְלַאכְתּוֹ, אֲשֶׁר־בָּרָא
אֱלֹהִים לַעֲשׂוֹת.

And there was evening and there was morning, the sixth day. And the heaven and the earth were finished, and all their host. And on the seventh day God finished work that had been done; and God rested on the seventh day from all the work that had been done. And God blessed the seventh day, and sanctified it; because that one day was the rest day from all the divine work that God created in doing (Genesis 1:31–2:3).

If the Seder is on a weeknight, begin here:

סַבְרִי מָרָנָן וְרַבָּנָן וְרַבּוֹתַי. בָּרוּךְ אַתָּה יְיָ, אֱלֹהֵינוּ מֶלֶךְ הָעוֹלָם,
בּוֹרֵא פְּרִי הַגָּפֶן. בָּרוּךְ אַתָּה יְיָ, אֱלֹהֵינוּ מֶלֶךְ הָעוֹלָם, אֲשֶׁר בָּחַר
בָּנוּ מִכָּל־עָם, וְרוֹמְמָנוּ מִכָּל־לָשׁוֹן, וְקִדְּשָׁנוּ בְּמִצְוֹתָיו, וַתִּתֶּן־
לָנוּ יְיָ אֱלֹהֵינוּ בְּאַהֲבָה (on shabbat add שַׁבָּתוֹת לִמְנוּחָה וּ)
מוֹעֲדִים לְשִׂמְחָה, חַגִּים וּזְמַנִּים לְשָׂשׂוֹן אֶת־יוֹם
(on shabbat add הַשַּׁבָּת הַזֶּה וְאֶת־יוֹם) חַג הַמַּצּוֹת הַזֶּה. זְמַן
חֵרוּתֵנוּ, (on shabbat add בְּאַהֲבָה,) מִקְרָא קֹדֶשׁ, זֵכֶר לִיצִיאַת
מִצְרָיִם. כִּי בָנוּ בָחַרְתָּ וְאוֹתָנוּ קִדַּשְׁתָּ מִכָּל־הָעַמִּים.
(on shabbat add וְשַׁבָּת) וּמוֹעֲדֵי קָדְשֶׁךָ (on shabbat add בְּאַהֲבָה
וּבְרָצוֹן) בְּשִׂמְחָה וּבְשָׂשׂוֹן הִנְחַלְתָּנוּ. בָּרוּךְ אַתָּה יְיָ, מְקַדֵּשׁ
(on shabbat add הַשַּׁבָּת וְ) יִשְׂרָאֵל וְהַזְּמַנִּים.

Praised are You, our God, Sovereign of the Universe, who creates the fruit of the vine. Praised are You, our God, Sovereign of the Universe, who has chosen us from all peoples and has raised us above all tongues and has sanctified us with the divine commandments. And You have given us, our God, [Sabbaths for rest], appointed times for happiness, holidays, and special times for joy, [this Sabbath day, and] this Festival of Matzot, our season of freedom [in love], a holy convocation, in memory of the Exodus from Egypt. For You have chosen us and sanctified us above all peoples. In Your gracious love, You granted us Your [holy Sabbath, and] special times for happiness and joy. Praised are You, our God, who sanctifies [the Sabbath,] Israel, and the appointed times.

If the Seder is on a Saturday night, add Havdalah:

בָּרוּךְ אַתָּה יְיָ, אֱלֹהֵינוּ מֶלֶךְ הָעוֹלָם, בּוֹרֵא מְאוֹרֵי הָאֵשׁ. בָּרוּךְ אַתָּה יְיָ, אֱלֹהֵינוּ מֶלֶךְ הָעוֹלָם, הַמַּבְדִּיל בֵּין קֹדֶשׁ לְחֹל בֵּין אוֹר לְחֹשֶׁךְ, בֵּין יִשְׂרָאֵל לָעַמִּים, בֵּין יוֹם הַשְּׁבִיעִי לְשֵׁשֶׁת יְמֵי הַמַּעֲשֶׂה. בֵּין קְדֻשַּׁת שַׁבָּת לִקְדֻשַּׁת יוֹם טוֹב הִבְדַּלְתָּ. וְאֶת-יוֹם הַשְּׁבִיעִי מִשֵּׁשֶׁת יְמֵי הַמַּעֲשֶׂה קִדַּשְׁתָּ. הִבְדַּלְתָּ וְקִדַּשְׁתָּ אֶת-עַמְּךָ יִשְׂרָאֵל בִּקְדֻשָּׁתֶךָ. בָּרוּךְ אַתָּה יְיָ, הַמַּבְדִּיל בֵּין קֹדֶשׁ לְקֹדֶשׁ.

בָּרוּךְ אַתָּה יְיָ, אֱלֹהֵינוּ מֶלֶךְ הָעוֹלָם, שֶׁהֶחֱיָנוּ וְקִיְּמָנוּ וְהִגִּיעָנוּ לַזְּמַן הַזֶּה.

Praised are You, our God, Sovereign of the Universe, who creates the light of the fire. Praised are You, our God, Sovereign of the Universe, who distinguishes between the holy and the profane, between light and darkness, between Israel and the nations, between the seventh day and the six working days. You have distinguished between the holiness of the Sabbath and the holiness of the Festival, and You have sanctified the seventh day above the six working days. You have distinguished and sanctified Your people Israel with Your holiness. Praised are You, God, who distinguishes between the holy and the holy.

Praised are You, our God, Sovereign of the Universe, who has granted us life and sustained us and brought us to this special time.

19

Kiddush (to make holy): What was one holy moment in your journey this year?

everyone

Wine brings out our love and passion. What part of the Exodus story do you love?

20

Urchatz ○ וּרְחַץ ○ Washing Hands

Ritually wash hands without reciting the blessing.

Karpas ○ כַּרְפַּס ○ Vegetable

Take from the greens; dip into the saltwater. The blessing on this vegetable is the same as for the bitter herb that we will eat in a few moments, so when you say the blessing "who creates the fruit of the earth," have the bitter herb in mind as well. Eat without reclining.

בָּרוּךְ אַתָּה יְיָ, אֱלֹהֵינוּ מֶלֶךְ הָעוֹלָם,
בּוֹרֵא פְּרִי הָאֲדָמָה.

Praised are You, our God, Sovereign of the Universe, who creates the fruit of the earth.

Karpas

Is there really any reason for a sprig of parsley to be on the Seder table? What is the connection between *karpas* and the Jewish People leaving Egypt?

Winter, with its bleak landscape and cold, short days, can lead to gloom and despondency.

In contrast, spring breeds hope. Seeds frozen in the earth rested over the winter. Now, in the spring, they awaken. Even when all is cold and dark, the indomitable force of life works beneath the surface, eventually bringing new flowers into the light of day. The first growth of spring, the first green stem to rise up, renews our trust in the stubborn and invincible force of life.

We begin the Seder by eating *karpas*, a breath of spring. With it, we ingest the resolute force of new life. Its color, smell, and taste remind us of the tough power of life within. We are eating the hope of nature itself.

What aspect of the natural world gives you hope? What is the most hopeful place you have ever been?

21

Yachatz ○ יַחַץ ○ Breaking the Middle Matzah

Take the middle matzah and break it into two, one piece larger than the other.
The larger piece is set aside to serve as the *afikoman*. The smaller piece is put back between the two matzot.

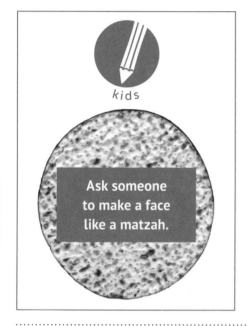

kids

Ask someone
to make a face
like a matzah.

one on one

Yachatz

At the beginning of the Seder we break the matzah and hide a piece away for the *afikoman* at the end of the Seder. We start the Seder with brokenness, with a piece missing. We are never really ready to begin our journey. There is always some brokenness; there is always a piece missing. It is risky to venture into the unknown without assurances that everything will work out. There are always good reasons for staying put.

Right after *yachatz* we say, "*Ha lachma onya*." "Now we are here, next year may we observe Passover in the land of Israel; this year many are still enslaved, next year may we all be free people." We have a vision. We have a mission. Despite the good reasons for staying put, the brokenness, and the pieces missing, we begin our journey. It is an act of defiant courage.

At every stage in our lives we can choose between remaining stuck and risking moving ahead.

What was the risk you took in the past year (or years) on your journey? What was the missing piece you found for last year's journey? What is risky about the next step on your journey?

Maggid · מַגִּיד · Retelling the Passover Story

Uncover the matzot, raise the Seder plate, and say:

הָא לַחְמָא עַנְיָא דִי אֲכָלוּ אַבְהָתָנָא בְּאַרְעָא
דְמִצְרָיִם. כָּל דִכְפִין יֵיתֵי וְיֵיכֹל, כָּל דִצְרִיךְ יֵיתֵי
וְיִפְסַח. הָשַׁתָּא הָכָא, לְשָׁנָה הַבָּאָה בְּאַרְעָא
דְיִשְׂרָאֵל. הָשַׁתָּא עַבְדֵי, לְשָׁנָה הַבָּאָה בְּנֵי חוֹרִין.

This is the bread of poverty that our ancestors ate in the land of Egypt. Anyone who is hungry should come and eat; all who are needy should come and celebrate Passover with us. Now we are here, next year may we observe Passover in the land of Israel; this year many are still enslaved, next year may we all be free people.

The tray with the matzot is moved aside, and the second cup is poured. (Do not drink it yet.)

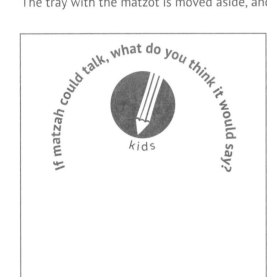

If matzah could talk, what do you think it would say?

kids

everyone

Kol Dichfin (anyone who is hungry): **Who would you want to invite to your Seder?**

23

hope-giver

"Anyone Who Is Hungry"

We are hardwired to give. One of the worst feelings in the world is not being needed by others.

But a slave has nothing to offer. Drained of energy and time, the slave's emotional and physical resources are depleted. With no ability to give, slaves lose their sense of humanity, feel empty and worthless, and incapable of generosity.

So we begin the Seder by proclaiming, "Anyone who is hungry should come and eat!" We are no longer slaves with nothing to give. No matter what our situation, we boldly declare that we have food in abundance and that we can't wait to share it with the world—a moment of exaggerated and piercing "largeness."

This sentence—"Anyone who is hungry should come and eat"—should not be read. It should be screamed! It is announcing, "I am a giving person! I am overflowing with goodness and kindness! I have a full tank of giving to share with everyone!"

Share a moment when you either carried out or witnessed a momentous act of extraordinary giving.

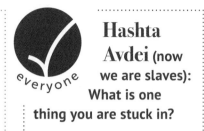

everyone

Hashta Avdei (now we are slaves): **What is one thing you are stuck in?**

24

Pour the second cup of wine. Now the child asks, "*Mah Nishtanah?*"

מַה נִּשְׁתַּנָּה הַלַּיְלָה הַזֶּה מִכָּל הַלֵּילוֹת?

What makes this night different from all other nights?

○ שֶׁבְּכָל **הַלֵּילוֹת** אָנוּ אוֹכְלִין חָמֵץ וּמַצָּה. הַלַּיְלָה הַזֶּה כֻּלּוֹ מַצָּה.

○ **On all other nights** we eat *chametz* and matzah. Why tonight, only matzah?

○ שֶׁבְּכָל **הַלֵּילוֹת** אָנוּ אוֹכְלִין שְׁאָר יְרָקוֹת הַלַּיְלָה הַזֶּה מָרוֹר.

○ **On all other nights** we eat other vegetables. Why tonight specifically maror (bitter herb)?

○ שֶׁבְּכָל **הַלֵּילוֹת** אֵין אָנוּ מַטְבִּילִין אֲפִילוּ פַּעַם אֶחָת. הַלַּיְלָה הַזֶּה שְׁתֵּי פְעָמִים.

○ **On all other nights** we don't dip our food even one time, but tonight we dip it twice?!

○ שֶׁבְּכָל **הַלֵּילוֹת** אָנוּ אוֹכְלִין בֵּין יוֹשְׁבִין וּבֵין מְסֻבִּין. הַלַּיְלָה הַזֶּה כֻּלָּנוּ מְסֻבִּין.

○ **On all other nights** we eat either sitting or reclining. Why tonight do we all recline?

kids

If maror (the bitter herb) could talk, what do you think it would say?

25

hope-giver

Mah Nishtanah—Making Changes

The life of a slave never changes. The clothes are the same. The food is the same. The routine is the same.

At the very beginning of the Seder, we ask the question, *Mah nishtanah ha'lailah hazeh?* "What makes this night different?"

We could have asked the same question during Succot, when we sleep outside in a fragile booth. Or on Purim when we put on masks and drink all day. Why on Passover do we emphasize difference?

Because, in a nutshell, Passover itself is change. On Passover, we move—we *pass over*—from slavery to freedom. We're not stuck. We're not trapped. We can control our lives and change what we want to change.

Every child learns *Mah Nishtanah*. We even ask our youngest children, before they have any experience of life, to recite it. It is our secret code. From the earliest stages we have to embed it deep inside: we are free; we can be different.

Mah Nishtanah **is the song of hope.** Things can be different. We are slaves no longer.

Make your Seder table different this year. Put something new on it—sparkles, chocolates, a gimmick, or props. What would you choose?

26

Return the plate to the table. The matzot should be uncovered during the "story-telling" of the haggadah.

עֲבָדִים הָיִינוּ לְפַרְעֹה בְּמִצְרָיִם. וַיּוֹצִיאֵנוּ יְיָ אֱלֹהֵינוּ מִשָּׁם, בְּיָד חֲזָקָה וּבִזְרוֹעַ נְטוּיָה, וְאִלּוּ לֹא הוֹצִיא הַקָּדוֹשׁ בָּרוּךְ הוּא אֶת־אֲבוֹתֵינוּ מִמִּצְרַיִם, הֲרֵי אָנוּ וּבָנֵינוּ וּבְנֵי בָנֵינוּ, מְשֻׁעְבָּדִים הָיִינוּ לְפַרְעֹה בְּמִצְרָיִם. וַאֲפִילוּ כֻּלָּנוּ חֲכָמִים, כֻּלָּנוּ נְבוֹנִים, כֻּלָּנוּ זְקֵנִים, כֻּלָּנוּ יוֹדְעִים אֶת־הַתּוֹרָה, מִצְוָה עָלֵינוּ לְסַפֵּר בִּיצִיאַת מִצְרָיִם. וְכָל הַמַּרְבֶּה לְסַפֵּר בִּיצִיאַת מִצְרָיִם, הֲרֵי זֶה מְשֻׁבָּח.

We were once slaves to Pharaoh in the land of Egypt, but our God took us out from there with a strong hand and an outstretched arm. Had the Holy One, praised be God, not taken our ancestors from Egypt, then we and our children and our children's children might still be enslaved to Pharaoh in Egypt. Therefore, even if we were all endowed with wisdom and understanding, all thoroughly versed in Torah, it would nevertheless still be necessary for us to tell the story of the Exodus from Egypt. And to invest more time describing this liberation from Egypt is indeed praiseworthy.

kids

Can you summarize the Exodus in one sentence?
If you could only send a ten-word text message about leaving Egypt, what would you say?

מַעֲשֶׂה בְּרַבִּי אֱלִיעֶזֶר, וְרַבִּי יְהוֹשֻׁעַ, וְרַבִּי אֶלְעָזָר בֶּן עֲזַרְיָה, וְרַבִּי עֲקִיבָא, וְרַבִּי טַרְפוֹן, שֶׁהָיוּ מְסֻבִּין בִּבְנֵי־בְרַק, וְהָיוּ מְסַפְּרִים בִּיצִיאַת מִצְרַיִם, כָּל־אוֹתוֹ הַלַּיְלָה, עַד שֶׁבָּאוּ תַלְמִידֵיהֶם וְאָמְרוּ לָהֶם. רַבּוֹתֵינוּ, הִגִּיעַ זְמַן קְרִיאַת שְׁמַע, שֶׁל שַׁחֲרִית.

We are told that Rabbi Eliezer, Rabbi Yehoshua, Rabbi Elazar ben Azariah, Rabbi Akiva, and Rabbi Tarfon were sitting at the Seder table in B'nei Brak and throughout the whole night discussed the Exodus from Egypt—until their students came and said to them, "Rabbis! It is already time to recite the Shema of the morning prayers!"

hope-giver

Soul Mates—Talking Till Morning

A slave doesn't have much to talk about. There are no personal goals, no dreams or aspirations, no highlights, and no change. Just the same old, same old.

And with nothing to talk about, there isn't much hope for deep friendship. There is nothing new to share. Being a slave is a very lonely experience.

On the other hand, people who talk till sunrise are full of passion and hope. We simply don't want to go to sleep. Our conversation keeps pushing us for more; we are oblivious to our need for rest.

People who are in love—whether with another person or a project—stay up all night talking. There is so much to know; there is endless curiosity and interest.

The rabbis sat together till the sun came up. They couldn't stop. They had found their fellow travelers.

Who are your traveling partners? With whom could you talk till dawn? What is one idea you would talk about?

אָמַר רַבִּי אֶלְעָזָר בֶּן־עֲזַרְיָה. הֲרֵי אֲנִי כְּבֶן שִׁבְעִים שָׁנָה, וְלֹא זָכִיתִי, שֶׁתֵּאָמֵר יְצִיאַת מִצְרַיִם בַּלֵּילוֹת. עַד שֶׁדְּרָשָׁהּ בֶּן זוֹמָא. שֶׁנֶּאֱמַר: לְמַעַן תִּזְכֹּר, אֶת יוֹם צֵאתְךָ מֵאֶרֶץ מִצְרַיִם, כֹּל יְמֵי חַיֶּיךָ. יְמֵי חַיֶּיךָ הַיָּמִים. כֹּל יְמֵי חַיֶּיךָ הַלֵּילוֹת.

וַחֲכָמִים אוֹמְרִים: יְמֵי חַיֶּיךָ הָעוֹלָם הַזֶּה. כֹּל יְמֵי חַיֶּיךָ לְהָבִיא לִימוֹת הַמָּשִׁיחַ.

בָּרוּךְ הַמָּקוֹם. בָּרוּךְ הוּא. בָּרוּךְ שֶׁנָּתַן תּוֹרָה לְעַמּוֹ יִשְׂרָאֵל.

בָּרוּךְ הוּא כְּנֶגֶד אַרְבָּעָה בָנִים דִּבְּרָה תוֹרָה. אֶחָד חָכָם, וְאֶחָד רָשָׁע, וְאֶחָד תָּם, וְאֶחָד שֶׁאֵינוֹ יוֹדֵעַ לִשְׁאוֹל.

Rabbi Elazar ben Azariah said, "I am nearly seventy years old and I did not understand why the Exodus from Egypt should be mentioned in both the morning and evening prayers, until Ben Zoma explained according to the verse, 'That you may remember the day you went forth from Egypt all the days of your life' (Deuteronomy 16:3). Had the verse only said 'the days of your life,' this would imply that leaving Egypt should be mentioned during the daytime. Since it says 'all the days of your life' this includes the nights as well."

The Sages offer another explanation: "'The days of your life' refers to speaking of the Exodus during this world. 'All the days of your life' includes the Messianic era."

Praised be God; praised be the Divine. Praised be the One who gave the Torah specifically to the people of Israel, praised be God.

The Torah speaks about four kinds of children. One is wise, one is rebellious, one is innocent, and one doesn't know how to ask.

everyone

Today, what questions do you imagine the wise child would ask?

חָכָם מַה הוּא אוֹמֵר? מָה הָעֵדֹת וְהַחֻקִּים וְהַמִּשְׁפָּטִים, אֲשֶׁר צִוָּה יְיָ אֱלֹהֵינוּ אֶתְכֶם? וְאַף אַתָּה אֱמָר־לוֹ כְּהִלְכוֹת הַפֶּסַח: אֵין מַפְטִירִין אַחַר הַפֶּסַח אֲפִיקוֹמָן:

רָשָׁע מַה הוּא אוֹמֵר? מָה הָעֲבֹדָה הַזֹּאת לָכֶם? לָכֶם וְלֹא לוֹ. וּלְפִי שֶׁהוֹצִיא אֶת־עַצְמוֹ מִן הַכְּלָל, כָּפַר בָּעִקָּר. וְאַף אַתָּה הַקְהֵה אֶת־שִׁנָּיו, וֶאֱמָר־לוֹ: בַּעֲבוּר זֶה עָשָׂה יְיָ לִי בְּצֵאתִי מִמִּצְרָיִם, לִי וְלֹא־לוֹ. אִלּוּ הָיָה שָׁם, לֹא הָיָה נִגְאָל.

תָּם מַה הוּא אוֹמֵר? מַה זֹּאת? וְאָמַרְתָּ אֵלָיו: בְּחֹזֶק יָד הוֹצִיאָנוּ יְיָ מִמִּצְרַיִם מִבֵּית עֲבָדִים.

וְשֶׁאֵינוֹ יוֹדֵעַ לִשְׁאוֹל, אַתְּ פְּתַח לוֹ. שֶׁנֶּאֱמַר: וְהִגַּדְתָּ לְבִנְךָ בַּיּוֹם הַהוּא לֵאמֹר: בַּעֲבוּר זֶה עָשָׂה יְיָ לִי, בְּצֵאתִי מִמִּצְרָיִם.

The wise child asks, "What are these testimonies, statutes, and ordinances that our God commanded you?" (Deuteronomy 6:20). You should explain to this child the laws of the Passover offering even to the last detail—that no dessert may be eaten after we are finished eating the *afikoman* (Mishnah Pesachim 10:8).

The rebellious child asks, "What is this worship to you?" (Exodus 12:26). By saying "to you," the child excludes him/herself from the rest of the nation. You should respond accordingly with a caustic answer: "It is because of what God did *for me* going out of Egypt" (Exodus 13:8), emphasizing "for me," because if the rebellious child had been there, s/he would not have been saved.

The innocent child asks, "What is this?" (Exodus 13:14). Tell the child, "With a strong hand, God took us out from Egypt, from the house of slaves" (Exodus 13:14).

As for the one who doesn't know to ask, you should begin by explaining, as we are told, "You shall tell your son on that day, 'I do this because of what God did for me when I left Egypt'" (Exodus 13:8).

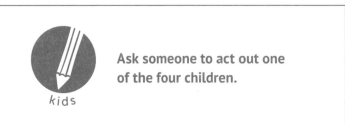

Ask someone to act out one of the four children.

kids

30

seniors

Tell us about your Seder when you were a kid. What stands out?

31

everyone

Four children, four different kinds of responses. What would be the most helpful question someone could ask you about your journey?

everyone

Chacham (the wise child): **What is one smart thing you did on your journey?**

Kids

Pharaoh declared that every male Jewish baby should be thrown into the Nile.

According to the Midrash, the despairing Jews in Egypt wanted to quit having children. Why bring a child into this world if the child's fate would be so tragic and heartbreaking? The Jews had lost hope in the future and chose not to have kids.

In contrast, our Seder is totally focused on children. We get *naches* when our little ones sing "*Mah Nishtanah.*" And who doesn't think of the four children when thinking about the Seder?

When I ask people, "What gives you hope?" the most common answer I receive is "kids." Hardships wear us down, but kids come along to spark and resuscitate our optimism.

Teaching our children the story of Passover is our declaration of hope in the future.

Where is the kid in you? Would you like to be more "kid-ish"? What part of you still has a child's unbridled optimism?

33

יָכוֹל מֵרֹאשׁ חֹדֶשׁ, תַּלְמוּד לוֹמַר בַּיּוֹם הַהוּא. אִי בַּיּוֹם הַהוּא. יָכוֹל מִבְּעוֹד יוֹם. תַּלְמוּד לוֹמַר. בַּעֲבוּר זֶה. בַּעֲבוּר זֶה לֹא אָמַרְתִּי, אֶלָּא בְּשָׁעָה שֶׁיֵּשׁ מַצָּה וּמָרוֹר מֻנָּחִים לְפָנֶיךָ.

מִתְּחִלָּה עוֹבְדֵי עֲבוֹדָה זָרָה הָיוּ אֲבוֹתֵינוּ. וְעַכְשָׁו קֵרְבָנוּ הַמָּקוֹם לַעֲבוֹדָתוֹ. שֶׁנֶּאֱמַר: וַיֹּאמֶר יְהוֹשֻׁעַ אֶל־כָּל־הָעָם. כֹּה אָמַר יְיָ אֱלֹהֵי יִשְׂרָאֵל, בְּעֵבֶר הַנָּהָר יָשְׁבוּ אֲבוֹתֵיכֶם מֵעוֹלָם, תֶּרַח אֲבִי אַבְרָהָם וַאֲבִי נָחוֹר. וַיַּעַבְדוּ אֱלֹהִים אֲחֵרִים. וָאֶקַּח אֶת־אֲבִיכֶם אֶת־אַבְרָהָם מֵעֵבֶר הַנָּהָר, וָאוֹלֵךְ אוֹתוֹ בְּכָל־אֶרֶץ כְּנָעַן. וָאַרְבֶּה אֶת־זַרְעוֹ, וָאֶתֶּן לוֹ אֶת־יִצְחָק. וָאֶתֵּן לְיִצְחָק אֶת־יַעֲקֹב וְאֶת־עֵשָׂו. וָאֶתֵּן לְעֵשָׂו אֶת־הַר שֵׂעִיר, לָרֶשֶׁת אוֹתוֹ. וְיַעֲקֹב וּבָנָיו יָרְדוּ מִצְרָיִם.

בָּרוּךְ שׁוֹמֵר הַבְטָחָתוֹ לְיִשְׂרָאֵל. בָּרוּךְ הוּא. שֶׁהַקָּדוֹשׁ בָּרוּךְ הוּא חִשַּׁב אֶת־הַקֵּץ, לַעֲשׂוֹת כְּמָה שֶׁאָמַר לְאַבְרָהָם אָבִינוּ בִּבְרִית בֵּין הַבְּתָרִים, שֶׁנֶּאֱמַר: וַיֹּאמֶר לְאַבְרָם יָדֹעַ תֵּדַע, כִּי־גֵר יִהְיֶה זַרְעֲךָ, בְּאֶרֶץ לֹא לָהֶם, וַעֲבָדוּם וְעִנּוּ אֹתָם אַרְבַּע מֵאוֹת שָׁנָה. וְגַם אֶת־הַגּוֹי אֲשֶׁר יַעֲבֹדוּ דָּן אָנֹכִי. וְאַחֲרֵי כֵן יֵצְאוּ בִּרְכֻשׁ גָּדוֹל.

Cover the matzah, lift the cup, and say:

וְהִיא שֶׁעָמְדָה לַאֲבוֹתֵינוּ וְלָנוּ. שֶׁלֹּא אֶחָד בִּלְבָד עָמַד עָלֵינוּ לְכַלּוֹתֵנוּ. אֶלָּא שֶׁבְּכָל דּוֹר וָדוֹר עוֹמְדִים עָלֵינוּ לְכַלּוֹתֵנוּ. וְהַקָּדוֹשׁ בָּרוּךְ הוּא מַצִּילֵנוּ מִיָּדָם.

One might think that the haggadah should be recited beginning from the first day of the month of Nisan. But the Torah says that you should tell your children "on that day," meaning the fifteenth of Nisan, the first day of Passover. Perhaps "on that day" is meant to teach that the haggadah should be recited during the daytime! But the verse continues, "I do this because of what God did for me when I left Egypt." "This" is the matzah and bitter herb actually resting on the Seder plate in front of you.

In the beginning, our ancestors were idol worshipers. Now, God has brought us into personal service, as we learn in the Torah: "Yehoshua said to the whole nation, 'Thus said the God of Israel, your ancestors used to live on the other side of the river Euphrates; Terach, the father of Abraham and the father of Nachor. They worshiped idols. But I took your father Abraham from beyond the river and I made him walk throughout the land of Canaan. I multiplied his offspring and I gave him Isaac. To Isaac, I gave Jacob and Esau. To Esau I gave Mount Seir as an inheritance; but Jacob and his sons went down to Egypt.'"

Praised is the One who keeps earlier promises to Israel, praised be God! The Holy One, who shall be praised, determined the end of our bondage in order to keep as was promised in a covenant with our father Abraham: "And God said to Abram, 'Know this for sure: your descendants will be a stranger in a land not their own, where they will be enslaved and oppressed for four hundred years. But I will bring judgment on the nation that oppressed them, and in the end they will go free with great wealth'" (Genesis 15:13–14).

God's unfailing help has stood for our ancestors and for us. It is not only that one enemy has risen up to destroy us; but in every generation, they stand up to destroy us. Yet the Holy One, who shall be praised, rescues us from their hands.

A Spiritual Cavalry

As if our suffering in Egypt were not enough, at the Seder we proclaim, "In every generation, they stand up to destroy us."

Ugh. Really? In every generation??

There is no smooth and easy road for the Jewish People.

In our own lifetimes, we have experienced war, terrorism, and anti-Semitism. According to the haggadah, these hardships and disasters will never end. We are bonded with adversity.

Yet the haggadah also promises that God will rescue us from the forces of destruction. The Jewish People will survive. Our entire history demonstrates that deliverance comes just when we think all is lost.

Did you notice any moment in the past year when you felt the hand of God helping the Jewish People?

35

Put down the cup and uncover the matzah.

צֵא וּלְמַד, מַה בִּקֵּשׁ לָבָן הָאֲרַמִּי לַעֲשׂוֹת לְיַעֲקֹב אָבִינוּ. שֶׁפַּרְעֹה לֹא גָזַר אֶלָּא עַל הַזְּכָרִים, וְלָבָן בִּקֵּשׁ לַעֲקֹר אֶת־הַכֹּל, שֶׁנֶּאֱמַר: אֲרַמִּי אֹבֵד אָבִי, וַיֵּרֶד מִצְרַיְמָה, וַיָּגָר שָׁם בִּמְתֵי מְעָט. וַיְהִי שָׁם לְגוֹי גָּדוֹל, עָצוּם וָרָב.

Let us study what Laban the Aramean sought to do to Jacob, our father. Pharaoh only decreed death for the males, but Laban sought to annihilate Jacob and his whole lineage. Supporting this interpretation, the biblical verse (in Deuteronomy 26:5) may be understood as, "An Aramean wanted to destroy my father." [What follows is a midrashic interpretation of the following verse:] "An Aramean wanted to destroy my father but he went down to Egypt. He resided there as a small tribe and there he became a nation, great and mighty and numerous."

וַיֵּרֶד מִצְרַיְמָה, אָנוּס עַל פִּי הַדִּבּוּר. וַיָּגָר שָׁם. מְלַמֵּד שֶׁלֹּא יָרַד יַעֲקֹב אָבִינוּ לְהִשְׁתַּקֵּעַ בְּמִצְרַיִם, אֶלָּא לָגוּר שָׁם, שֶׁנֶּאֱמַר: וַיֹּאמְרוּ אֶל־פַּרְעֹה, לָגוּר בָּאָרֶץ בָּאנוּ, כִּי אֵין מִרְעֶה לַצֹּאן אֲשֶׁר לַעֲבָדֶיךָ, כִּי כָבֵד הָרָעָב בְּאֶרֶץ כְּנָעַן. וְעַתָּה, יֵשְׁבוּ־נָא עֲבָדֶיךָ בְּאֶרֶץ גֹּשֶׁן.

"He went down to Egypt"—compelled by divine command. "He resided there"—from which we learn that Jacob didn't intend to settle in Egypt but only to dwell there temporarily, as we learn in the Torah: "Jacob's sons said to Pharaoh, 'We would like to reside in Egypt since there is not enough pasture for our flocks in Canaan, as there is a severe famine there. Please let your servants dwell in the land of Goshen'" (Genesis 47:4).

kids

Ask someone to talk in Egyptian.

בִּמְתֵי מְעָט. כְּמָה שֶׁנֶּאֱמַר: בְּשִׁבְעִים נֶפֶשׁ יָרְדוּ אֲבֹתֶיךָ מִצְרַיְמָה. וְעַתָּה, שָׂמְךָ יְיָ אֱלֹהֶיךָ, כְּכוֹכְבֵי הַשָּׁמַיִם לָרֹב.

"A small tribe"—as Moses said to the Children of Israel, "With only seventy souls your ancestors came down to Egypt, but now your God has made you as numerous as the stars of the sky" (Deuteronomy 10:22).

וַיְהִי שָׁם לְגוֹי. מְלַמֵּד שֶׁהָיוּ יִשְׂרָאֵל מְצֻיָּנִים שָׁם.

"And there he became a nation"—indicating that even then the Israelites were identified as a unique people.

גָּדוֹל עָצוּם, כְּמָה שֶׁנֶּאֱמַר: וּבְנֵי יִשְׂרָאֵל פָּרוּ וַיִּשְׁרְצוּ, וַיִּרְבּוּ וַיַּעַצְמוּ, בִּמְאֹד מְאֹד, וַתִּמָּלֵא הָאָרֶץ אֹתָם.

"Great and mighty"—as we read, "And the Children of Israel were fruitful and increased abundantly and multiplied and grew great and mighty; and the land was full of them" (Exodus 1:7).

36

וָרָב. כְּמָה שֶׁנֶּאֱמַר: רְבָבָה כְּצֶמַח הַשָּׂדֶה נְתַתִּיךְ, וַתִּרְבִּי, וַתִּגְדְּלִי, וַתָּבֹאִי בַּעֲדִי עֲדָיִים. שָׁדַיִם נָכֹנוּ, וּשְׂעָרֵךְ צִמֵּחַ, וְאַתְּ עֵרֹם וְעֶרְיָה.

וָאֶעֱבֹר עָלַיִךְ וָאֶרְאֵךְ מִתְבּוֹסֶסֶת בְּדָמָיִךְ וָאֹמַר לָךְ בְּדָמַיִךְ חֲיִי וָאֹמַר לָךְ בְּדָמַיִךְ חֲיִי.

וַיָּרֵעוּ אֹתָנוּ הַמִּצְרִים וַיְעַנּוּנוּ. וַיִּתְּנוּ עָלֵינוּ עֲבֹדָה קָשָׁה. וַיָּרֵעוּ אֹתָנוּ הַמִּצְרִים. כְּמָה שֶׁנֶּאֱמַר: הָבָה נִתְחַכְּמָה לוֹ. פֶּן־יִרְבֶּה, וְהָיָה כִּי־תִקְרֶאנָה מִלְחָמָה, וְנוֹסַף גַּם הוּא עַל־שֹׂנְאֵינוּ, וְנִלְחַם־בָּנוּ וְעָלָה מִן־הָאָרֶץ.

וַיְעַנּוּנוּ. כְּמָה שֶׁנֶּאֱמַר: וַיָּשִׂימוּ עָלָיו שָׂרֵי מִסִּים, לְמַעַן עַנֹּתוֹ בְּסִבְלֹתָם. וַיִּבֶן עָרֵי מִסְכְּנוֹת לְפַרְעֹה, אֶת־פִּתֹם וְאֶת־רַעַמְסֵס. וַיִּתְּנוּ עָלֵינוּ עֲבֹדָה קָשָׁה. כְּמָה שֶׁנֶּאֱמַר: וַיַּעֲבִדוּ מִצְרַיִם אֶת־בְּנֵי יִשְׂרָאֵל בְּפָרֶךְ.

"And numerous"—as we read, "I have caused you to multiply as the buds of the field; and you did multiply and grow in beauty; your breasts were fashioned and your hair grew long; yet you remained naked and barren" (Ezekiel 16:7).

"And when I passed by you, and saw you wallowing in your blood, I said to you: In your blood, live; yes, I said to you: In your blood, live" (Ezekiel 16:6).

"And the Egyptians treated us harshly and oppressed us and imposed hard labor upon us" (Deuteronomy 26:6). "And the Egyptians treated us harshly"—indeed, Pharaoh said, "Come, let us outwit the Israelites, lest they multiply and, in the event that war breaks out, they will join our enemies and fight against us and escape Egypt" (Exodus 1:10).

"And oppressed us"—the Torah explains that "the Egyptians placed taskmasters over them to oppress them with heavy burdens; and they built treasure cities, Pitom and Ra'amses" (Exodus 1:11). "And imposed hard labor upon us"—as it is written, "The Egyptians imposed hard labor on the Children of Israel" (Exodus 1:11).

37

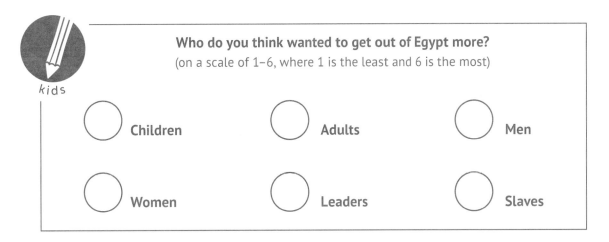

kids

Who do you think wanted to get out of Egypt more?
(on a scale of 1–6, where 1 is the least and 6 is the most)

◯ Children   ◯ Adults   ◯ Men

◯ Women   ◯ Leaders   ◯ Slaves

וַנִּצְעַק אֶל־יְיָ אֱלֹהֵי אֲבֹתֵינוּ, וַיִּשְׁמַע יְיָ אֶת־קֹלֵנוּ, וַיַּרְא אֶת־עָנְיֵנוּ, וְאֶת־עֲמָלֵנוּ, וְאֶת לַחֲצֵנוּ. וַנִּצְעַק אֶל־יְיָ אֱלֹהֵי אֲבֹתֵינוּ, כְּמָה שֶׁנֶּאֱמַר: וַיְהִי בַיָּמִים הָרַבִּים הָהֵם, וַיָּמָת מֶלֶךְ מִצְרַיִם, וַיֵּאָנְחוּ בְנֵי־יִשְׂרָאֵל מִן־הָעֲבֹדָה וַיִּזְעָקוּ. וַתַּעַל שַׁוְעָתָם אֶל־הָאֱלֹהִים מִן הָעֲבֹדָה.

"And we cried out to the God of our ancestors, and God heard our cry, and saw our affliction, and our travail and our duress" (Deuteronomy 26:7). "And we cried out to the God of our ancestors"—as we learn, "When many years had passed and the king of Egypt died, the Children of Israel moaned from their work and cried out, and from the midst of their slavery their supplication went up to God" (Exodus 2:23).

וַיִּשְׁמַע יְיָ אֶת־קֹלֵנוּ. כְּמָה שֶׁנֶּאֱמַר: וַיִּשְׁמַע אֱלֹהִים אֶת־נַאֲקָתָם, וַיִּזְכֹּר אֱלֹהִים אֶת־בְּרִיתוֹ, אֶת־אַבְרָהָם, אֶת־יִצְחָק, וְאֶת יַעֲקֹב.

"And God heard our cry"—as the verse elaborates, "God heard their groans and remembered the earlier covenant with Abraham, Isaac, and Jacob" (Exodus 2:24).

וַיַּרְא אֶת־עָנְיֵנוּ. זוֹ פְּרִישׁוּת דֶּרֶךְ אֶרֶץ. כְּמָה שֶׁנֶּאֱמַר: וַיַּרְא אֱלֹהִים אֶת־בְּנֵי יִשְׂרָאֵל. וַיֵּדַע אֱלֹהִים.

"And saw our affliction"—this refers to the forced separation of husbands and wives. This is hinted at in the verse, "God saw the Children of Israel and God knew their distress" (Exodus 2:25).

וְאֶת־עֲמָלֵנוּ. אֵלּוּ הַבָּנִים. כְּמָה שֶׁנֶּאֱמַר: כָּל־הַבֵּן הַיִּלּוֹד הַיְאֹרָה תַּשְׁלִיכֻהוּ, וְכָל־הַבַּת תְּחַיּוּן.

"And our travail"—this refers to the drowning of the sons, as it is written, "Every son that is born must be cast into the Nile, but every girl will be allowed to live" (Exodus 1:24).

וְאֶת לַחֲצֵנוּ. זֶה הַדְּחַק. כְּמָה שֶׁנֶּאֱמַר: וְגַם־רָאִיתִי אֶת־הַלַּחַץ, אֲשֶׁר מִצְרַיִם לֹחֲצִים אֹתָם.

"And our duress"—this refers to the oppression, as is written, "I have also seen the pressure that the Egyptians are applying on them" (Exodus 3:19).

וַיּוֹצִאֵנוּ יְיָ מִמִּצְרַיִם, בְּיָד חֲזָקָה, וּבִזְרֹעַ נְטוּיָה, וּבְמֹרָא גָּדֹל וּבְאֹתוֹת וּבְמֹפְתִים.

"And God took us out of Egypt with a strong hand and an outstretched arm in the midst of great awe, signs, and wonders" (Deuteronomy 26:8).

38

one on one

Every journey has its spiritual moment.

Taking steps on a journey, getting unstuck, always seems to have an element of mystery and the miraculous.

On your journey, was there ever a moment when you felt helped by God? Was there ever a moment that you sensed a deep spiritual connection to something beyond? What was that like for you?

39

וַיּוֹצִאֵנוּ יְיָ מִמִּצְרַיִם. לֹא עַל־יְדֵי מַלְאָךְ, וְלֹא עַל־יְדֵי שָׂרָף. וְלֹא עַל־יְדֵי שָׁלִיחַ. אֶלָּא הַקָּדוֹשׁ בָּרוּךְ הוּא בִּכְבוֹדוֹ וּבְעַצְמוֹ. שֶׁנֶּאֱמַר: וְעָבַרְתִּי בְאֶרֶץ מִצְרַיִם בַּלַּיְלָה הַזֶּה, וְהִכֵּיתִי כָל־בְּכוֹר בְּאֶרֶץ מִצְרַיִם, מֵאָדָם וְעַד בְּהֵמָה, וּבְכָל־אֱלֹהֵי מִצְרַיִם אֶעֱשֶׂה שְׁפָטִים אֲנִי יְיָ.

וְעָבַרְתִּי בְאֶרֶץ־מִצְרַיִם בַּלַּיְלָה הַזֶּה, אֲנִי וְלֹא מַלְאָךְ. וְהִכֵּיתִי כָל־בְּכוֹר בְּאֶרֶץ־מִצְרַיִם. אֲנִי וְלֹא שָׂרָף. וּבְכָל־אֱלֹהֵי מִצְרַיִם אֶעֱשֶׂה שְׁפָטִים, אֲנִי וְלֹא הַשָּׁלִיחַ. אֲנִי יְיָ, אֲנִי הוּא וְלֹא אַחֵר.

בְּיָד חֲזָקָה. זוֹ הַדֶּבֶר. כְּמָה שֶׁנֶּאֱמַר: הִנֵּה יַד־יְיָ הוֹיָה, בְּמִקְנְךָ אֲשֶׁר בַּשָּׂדֶה, בַּסּוּסִים בַּחֲמֹרִים בַּגְּמַלִּים, בַּבָּקָר וּבַצֹּאן, דֶּבֶר כָּבֵד מְאֹד.

וּבִזְרֹעַ נְטוּיָה. זוֹ הַחֶרֶב. כְּמָה שֶׁנֶּאֱמַר: וְחַרְבּוֹ שְׁלוּפָה בְּיָדוֹ, נְטוּיָה עַל־יְרוּשָׁלָיִם.

וּבְמֹרָא גָּדוֹל, זֶה גִּלּוּי שְׁכִינָה. כְּמָה שֶׁנֶּאֱמַר: אוֹ הֲנִסָּה אֱלֹהִים, לָבוֹא לָקַחַת לוֹ גוֹי מִקֶּרֶב גּוֹי, בְּמַסֹּת בְּאֹתֹת וּבְמוֹפְתִים וּבְמִלְחָמָה, וּבְיָד חֲזָקָה וּבִזְרוֹעַ נְטוּיָה, וּבְמוֹרָאִים גְּדֹלִים. כְּכֹל אֲשֶׁר־עָשָׂה לָכֶם יְיָ אֱלֹהֵיכֶם בְּמִצְרַיִם, לְעֵינֶיךָ.

וּבְאֹתוֹת. זֶה הַמַּטֶּה, כְּמָה שֶׁנֶּאֱמַר: וְאֶת הַמַּטֶּה הַזֶּה תִּקַּח בְּיָדֶךָ. אֲשֶׁר תַּעֲשֶׂה־בּוֹ אֶת־הָאֹתֹת.

וּבְמוֹפְתִים. זֶה הַדָּם. כְּמָה שֶׁנֶּאֱמַר: וְנָתַתִּי מוֹפְתִים, בַּשָּׁמַיִם וּבָאָרֶץ.

"And God took us out of Egypt"—not by any intermediary angel, seraph, or messenger, but by God in particular glory, the Holy One, praised be God, as the Torah teaches, "And I will pass through the land of Egypt on that night and I will smite every firstborn in the land of Egypt, both humans and beasts; and I will execute judgments against all the gods of Egypt, for I am God."

"And I will pass through the land of Egypt"—I and not an angel. "I will smite every firstborn"—I and not a seraph. "I will execute judgments against all the gods of Egypt"—I and not a messenger. "I am God"—that is I; there is no other.

"With a strong hand"—this refers to the cattle plague, as Pharaoh was warned, "Behold the hand of God will smite your herds in the field, your horses, donkeys, camels, cattle, and flocks; the plague will be severe indeed" (Exodus 9:3).

"And an outstretched arm"—this suggests destruction by sword, as we learn elsewhere, "And his sword was drawn in his hand, outstretched over Jerusalem" (1 Chronicles 21:16).

"In the midst of great awe"—this refers to the revelation of the Divine Presence. We understand this from the verse, "Has God ever tried to take for Himself a nation out of the midst of another nation by trials, signs, wonders, war, and by a mighty hand, outstretched arm, and with great and awesome acts, just as your God did for you, before your very eyes, in Egypt?" (Deuteronomy 4:34).

"Signs"—this alludes to the staff of Moses, as God said to Moses, "Take this staff in your hand, and with it you will perform the signs" (Exodus 4:17).

"Wonders"—this refers to the miracle where the water of the Nile turned into blood, hinted at in the verse, "I will show wonders in the heavens and on the earth" (Joel 3:3).

Spill a little wine from your cup while pronouncing each of these three miracles and the ten plagues below:

דָּם. וָאֵשׁ. וְתִימְרוֹת עָשָׁן.

"Blood. Fire. And pillars of smoke." (Joel 3:3)

דָּבָר אַחֵר. בְּיָד חֲזָקָה שְׁתַּיִם. וּבִזְרֹעַ
נְטוּיָה שְׁתַּיִם. וּבְמוֹרָא גָּדוֹל שְׁתַּיִם.
וּבְאֹתוֹת שְׁתַּיִם. וּבְמֹפְתִים שְׁתַּיִם.

Another interpretation (of Deuteronomy 26:8): "By a strong hand" indicates two plagues; "outstretched arm" indicates two plagues; "great awe" indicates two plagues; "signs" indicates two plagues; and "wonders" indicates two plagues.

אֵלּוּ עֶשֶׂר מַכּוֹת שֶׁהֵבִיא הַקָּדוֹשׁ בָּרוּךְ הוּא עַל־הַמִּצְרִים בְּמִצְרַיִם,
וְאֵלּוּ הֵן:

These are the ten plagues that the Holy One, blessed be God, brought upon the Egyptians in Egypt:

דָּם	Blood
צְפַרְדֵּעַ	Frogs
כִּנִּים	Lice
עָרוֹב	Wild Beasts
דֶּבֶר	Cattle Disease
שְׁחִין	Boils
בָּרָד	Hail
אַרְבֶּה	Locusts
חֹשֶׁךְ	Darkness
מַכַּת בְּכוֹרוֹת	Slaying of the Firstborn

kids

What do you think Pharaoh's kids were telling him during the ten plagues?

What was his wife saying to him?

everyone

Plagues: What has been "your plague" on your journey?

43

hope-giver

A Sense of Humor

I know that Passover, slavery, and redemption are serious topics. Everything was at stake for the Jewish People, and this is no laughing matter.

Yet I cannot help but smile when I think of the plague of frogs. Really? Frogs? Of all the frightening and disastrous plagues we could imagine, a mass of ribbeting, slimy, jumping frogs is probably not one of them.

The plague of blood is scary. Boils are gross. Darkness and locusts could be terrifying. But frogs?

Is it sacrilegious to suggest that God also has a sense of humor and wanted to offer the Jewish People a ridiculous and comic moment in the midst of their travail?

Have you ever been able to laugh while experiencing a difficult time? Does humor give you hope?

44

רַבִּי יְהוּדָה הָיָה נוֹתֵן בָּהֶם סִמָּנִים:

דְּצַ"ךְ

עֲדַ"שׁ

בְּאַחַ"ב

רַבִּי יוֹסֵי הַגְּלִילִי אוֹמֵר: מִנַּיִן אַתָּה אוֹמֵר שֶׁלָּקוּ הַמִּצְרִים בְּמִצְרַיִם עֶשֶׂר מַכּוֹת, וְעַל הַיָּם לָקוּ חֲמִשִּׁים מַכּוֹת? בְּמִצְרַיִם מָה הוּא אוֹמֵר: וַיֹּאמְרוּ הַחַרְטֻמִּם אֶל־פַּרְעֹה, אֶצְבַּע אֱלֹהִים הִוא. וְעַל הַיָּם מָה הוּא אוֹמֵר? וַיַּרְא יִשְׂרָאֵל אֶת־הַיָּד הַגְּדֹלָה, אֲשֶׁר עָשָׂה יְיָ בְּמִצְרַיִם, וַיִּירְאוּ הָעָם אֶת־יְיָ, וַיַּאֲמִינוּ בַּיְיָ, וּבְמֹשֶׁה עַבְדּוֹ. כַּמָּה לָקוּ בְּאֶצְבַּע, עֶשֶׂר מַכּוֹת. אֱמוֹר מֵעַתָּה, בְּמִצְרַיִם לָקוּ עֶשֶׂר מַכּוֹת, וְעַל־הַיָּם לָקוּ חֲמִשִּׁים מַכּוֹת.

רַבִּי אֱלִיעֶזֶר אוֹמֵר: מִנַּיִן שֶׁכָּל־מַכָּה וּמַכָּה, שֶׁהֵבִיא הַקָּדוֹשׁ בָּרוּךְ הוּא עַל הַמִּצְרִים בְּמִצְרַיִם, הָיְתָה שֶׁל אַרְבַּע מַכּוֹת? שֶׁנֶּאֱמַר: יְשַׁלַּח־בָּם חֲרוֹן אַפּוֹ, עֶבְרָה וָזַעַם וְצָרָה. מִשְׁלַחַת מַלְאֲכֵי רָעִים. עֶבְרָה אַחַת. וָזַעַם שְׁתַּיִם. וְצָרָה שָׁלֹשׁ. מִשְׁלַחַת מַלְאֲכֵי רָעִים אַרְבַּע. אֱמוֹר מֵעַתָּה, בְּמִצְרַיִם לָקוּ אַרְבָּעִים מַכּוֹת, וְעַל הַיָּם לָקוּ מָאתַיִם מַכּוֹת.

רַבִּי עֲקִיבָא אוֹמֵר: מִנַּיִן שֶׁכָּל־מַכָּה וּמַכָּה שֶׁהֵבִיא הַקָּדוֹשׁ בָּרוּךְ הוּא עַל הַמִּצְרִים בְּמִצְרַיִם הָיְתָה שֶׁל חָמֵשׁ מַכּוֹת? שֶׁנֶּאֱמַר: יְשַׁלַּח־בָּם חֲרוֹן אַפּוֹ, עֶבְרָה וָזַעַם וְצָרָה. מִשְׁלַחַת מַלְאֲכֵי רָעִים. חֲרוֹן אַפּוֹ אַחַת. עֶבְרָה שְׁתַּיִם. וָזַעַם שָׁלֹשׁ. וְצָרָה אַרְבַּע. מִשְׁלַחַת מַלְאֲכֵי רָעִים חָמֵשׁ. אֱמוֹר מֵעַתָּה, בְּמִצְרַיִם לָקוּ חֲמִשִּׁים מַכּוֹת, וְעַל הַיָּם לָקוּ חֲמִשִּׁים וּמָאתַיִם מַכּוֹת.

Rabbi Judah used to refer to the plagues as follows:

D'TZaKH [the Hebrew initials of the first three plagues];

ADaSH [the Hebrew initials of the second three plagues];

B'AHaB [the Hebrew initials of the last four plagues].

Rabbi Yossi, the Galilean, asked: How can one deduce that if the Egyptians were struck with ten plagues in Egypt, they were struck with fifty plagues at the Red Sea? Referring to the plagues in Egypt, the Torah says, "The magicians said to Pharaoh, 'This is the finger of God' (Exodus 8:15)." At the Red Sea, however, the Torah says, "And Israel saw the great hand which God laid upon the Egyptians, and the people stood in awe of God; and they believed in God, and the divine servant, Moses" (Exodus 14:31). If, in Egypt, the finger of God brought ten plagues, we may deduce that at the Red Sea the whole hand of God brought fifty plagues.

Rabbi Eliezer asked: How can one show that every plague that God brought upon the Egyptians was composed of four plagues? We are taught, "God sent against the Egyptians a fierce anger: wrath, fury, trouble, and messengers of evil" (Psalm 78:49). "Wrath" is the strength of one; "fury" makes two; "trouble" makes three; "messengers of evil" makes four. Therefore, if each plague is fourfold, in Egypt they were struck with forty plagues, and at the Red Sea they were struck with two hundred plagues.

Rabbi Akiva asked further: How can one infer that every plague that the Holy One, who should be praised, inflicted upon the Egyptians in Egypt was actually fivefold? "God sent against the Egyptians fierce anger, wrath, fury, trouble, and messengers of evil" (Psalm 78:49). "Fierce anger" is the strength of one; "wrath," twofold; "fury," threefold; "trouble," fourfold; "messengers of evil," fivefold. Therefore, if each plague is fivefold, in Egypt they were struck with fifty plagues, and at the Red Sea they were struck with two hundred and fifty plagues.

kids

If there weren't just ten plagues but fifty, what do you think some of the other plagues could have been? What plagues can you think of for today?

46

Every journey has moments worthy of exaggeration. Exaggeration makes the process more human and personal. Years from now, what moments in your journey do you think you will be exaggerating?

47

Dayenu ◦ דַּיֵּנוּ ◦ We Would Have Been Grateful!

כַּמָּה מַעֲלוֹת טוֹבוֹת לַמָּקוֹם עָלֵינוּ.

How thankful we should be to God for many deeds of kindness to us!

אִלּוּ הוֹצִיאָנוּ מִמִּצְרַיִם, וְלֹא עָשָׂה בָהֶם שְׁפָטִים, דַּיֵּנוּ.

Had God freed us from the Egyptians and not wrought judgment upon them, for that alone we would have been grateful!

אִלּוּ עָשָׂה בָהֶם שְׁפָטִים, וְלֹא עָשָׂה בֵאלֹהֵיהֶם, דַּיֵּנוּ.

Had God wrought judgment upon the Egyptians but not destroyed their gods, for that alone we would have been grateful!

אִלּוּ עָשָׂה בֵאלֹהֵיהֶם, וְלֹא הָרַג אֶת־בְּכוֹרֵיהֶם, דַּיֵּנוּ.

Had God destroyed their gods but not killed their firstborn children, for that alone we would have been grateful!

אִלּוּ הָרַג אֶת־בְּכוֹרֵיהֶם, וְלֹא נָתַן לָנוּ אֶת־מָמוֹנָם, דַּיֵּנוּ.

Had God killed their firstborn children but not given us their wealth, for that alone we would have been grateful!

אִלּוּ נָתַן לָנוּ אֶת־מָמוֹנָם, וְלֹא קָרַע לָנוּ אֶת־הַיָּם, דַּיֵּנוּ.

Had God given us their wealth but not split the Red Sea for us, for that alone we would have been grateful!

אִלּוּ קָרַע לָנוּ אֶת־הַיָּם, וְלֹא הֶעֱבִירָנוּ בְתוֹכוֹ בֶּחָרָבָה, דַּיֵּנוּ.

Had God split the Red Sea for us but not let us pass through it on dry land, for that alone we would have been grateful!

אִלּוּ הֶעֱבִירָנוּ בְתוֹכוֹ בֶּחָרָבָה, וְלֹא שִׁקַּע צָרֵינוּ בְּתוֹכוֹ, דַּיֵּנוּ.

Had God let us pass through the Sea on dry land but not drowned our enemies in it, for that alone we would have been grateful!

אִלּוּ שִׁקַּע צָרֵינוּ בְּתוֹכוֹ, וְלֹא סִפֵּק צָרְכֵּנוּ בַּמִּדְבָּר אַרְבָּעִים שָׁנָה, דַּיֵּנוּ.

Had God drowned our enemies in it but not supplied our needs in the wilderness for forty years, for that alone we would have been grateful!

אִלּוּ סִפֵּק צָרְכֵּנוּ בַּמִּדְבָּר אַרְבָּעִים שָׁנָה, וְלֹא הֶאֱכִילָנוּ אֶת־הַמָּן, דַּיֵּנוּ.

Had God supplied our needs in the wilderness for forty years but not fed us with manna, for that alone we would have been grateful!

אִלּוּ הֶאֱכִילָנוּ אֶת־הַמָּן, וְלֹא נָתַן לָנוּ אֶת־הַשַּׁבָּת, דַּיֵּנוּ.

Had God fed us with manna but not given us the Shabbat, for that alone we would have been grateful!

אִלּוּ נָתַן לָנוּ אֶת־הַשַּׁבָּת, וְלֹא קֵרְבָנוּ לִפְנֵי הַר סִינַי, דַּיֵּנוּ.

Had God given us the Shabbat but not brought us to Mount Sinai, for that alone we would have been grateful!

אִלּוּ קֵרְבָנוּ לִפְנֵי הַר סִינַי, וְלֹא נָתַן לָנוּ אֶת־הַתּוֹרָה, דַּיֵּנוּ.

Had God brought us to Mount Sinai but not given us the Torah, for that alone we would have been grateful!

אִלּוּ נָתַן לָנוּ אֶת־הַתּוֹרָה, וְלֹא הִכְנִיסָנוּ לְאֶרֶץ יִשְׂרָאֵל, דַּיֵּנוּ.

Had God given us the Torah but not brought us into the land of Israel, for that alone we would have been grateful!

אִלּוּ הִכְנִיסָנוּ לְאֶרֶץ יִשְׂרָאֵל, וְלֹא בָנָה לָנוּ אֶת־בֵּית הַבְּחִירָה, דַּיֵּנוּ.

Had God brought us into the land of Israel but not built us the Temple, for that alone we would have been grateful!

עַל אַחַת כַּמָּה וְכַמָּה טוֹבָה כְפוּלָה וּמְכֻפֶּלֶת לַמָּקוֹם עָלֵינוּ.

How much more so are we grateful to God for bestowing double and triple blessings upon us!

שֶׁהוֹצִיאָנוּ מִמִּצְרַיִם, וְעָשָׂה בָהֶם שְׁפָטִים, וְעָשָׂה בֵאלֹהֵיהֶם, וְהָרַג אֶת־בְּכוֹרֵיהֶם, וְנָתַן לָנוּ אֶת־מָמוֹנָם, וְקָרַע לָנוּ אֶת־הַיָּם, וְהֶעֱבִירָנוּ בְתוֹכוֹ בֶּחָרָבָה, וְשִׁקַּע צָרֵינוּ בְּתוֹכוֹ, וְסִפֵּק צָרְכֵּנוּ בַּמִּדְבָּר אַרְבָּעִים שָׁנָה, וְהֶאֱכִילָנוּ אֶת־הַמָּן, וְנָתַן לָנוּ אֶת־הַשַּׁבָּת, וְקֵרְבָנוּ לִפְנֵי הַר סִינַי, וְנָתַן לָנוּ אֶת־הַתּוֹרָה, וְהִכְנִיסָנוּ לְאֶרֶץ יִשְׂרָאֵל, וּבָנָה לָנוּ אֶת־בֵּית הַבְּחִירָה, לְכַפֵּר עַל־כָּל־עֲוֹנוֹתֵינוּ.

God freed us from the Egyptians and brought judgment upon them, God destroyed their gods, killed their firstborns, gave us their wealth, split the Sea for us, let us pass through it on dry land, drowned our enemies, supplied our needs in the wilderness for forty years, fed us with manna, gave us the Shabbat, brought us to Mount Sinai, gave us the Torah, brought us into the land of Israel, and built us the Temple where we can pray for the atonement of our sins.

everyone

Every journey has moments of gratitude—*Dayenu*. What are three specific moments of your journey worth singing about?

50

Expressing Gratitude

Sometimes the accumulation of life's small defeats can wear us down and make us lose hope.

My brain is flooded with, "Why didn't I do that? I can't believe I did that again; what on earth was I thinking?"

What would happen if I changed my focus? If instead of reminding myself of my failings, I started to list my successes? Even my little ones?

What would happen if we began publicizing achievements and blessings rather than catastrophes and setbacks?

What if we tried to see things in a positive light? If we constructed "gratitude lists" to make us more aware of all the wonderful things happening to us?

Singing the song "*Dayenu*," a keystone moment for many families, is nothing if not a "national gratitude list." After a rousing chorus, how can a person not have more hope?

What would be on your gratitude list for the Jewish People? Can you get to fifteen things?

51

רַבָּן גַּמְלִיאֵל הָיָה אוֹמֵר: כָּל שֶׁלֹּא אָמַר שְׁלֹשָׁה דְבָרִים אֵלּוּ בַּפֶּסַח, לֹא יָצָא יְדֵי חוֹבָתוֹ, וְאֵלּוּ הֵן:

Rabban Gamliel used to say, "Anyone who has not explained the following symbols of the Seder has not fulfilled the obligation:

פֶּסַח.   **Passover** (the paschal lamb).

מַצָּה.   **Matzah** (the unleavened bread).

וּמָרוֹר.   And **Maror** (the bitter herb)."

One of the participants asks:

פֶּסַח שֶׁהָיוּ אֲבוֹתֵינוּ אוֹכְלִים בִּזְמַן שֶׁבֵּית הַמִּקְדָּשׁ הָיָה קַיָם, עַל שׁוּם מָה? עַל שׁוּם שֶׁפָּסַח הַקָּדוֹשׁ בָּרוּךְ הוּא עַל בָּתֵּי אֲבוֹתֵינוּ בְּמִצְרַיִם, שֶׁנֶּאֱמַר: וַאֲמַרְתֶּם זֶבַח פֶּסַח הוּא לַיָי, אֲשֶׁר פָּסַח עַל בָּתֵּי בְנֵי יִשְׂרָאֵל בְּמִצְרַיִם, בְּנָגְפּוֹ אֶת־מִצְרַיִם וְאֶת־בָּתֵּינוּ הִצִּיל, וַיִּקֹּד הָעָם וַיִּשְׁתַּחֲווּ.

What is the meaning of the Passover sacrifice that our ancestors used to eat when the Temple was in existence? The Passover sacrifice was to remind us that the Holy One, who should be praised, passed over the homes of our ancestors in Egypt and did not kill our firstborn, as we read: "You shall say, 'It is the sacrifice of God's passing-over, for that God passed over the homes of the Children of Israel in Egypt, when the Egyptians were punished, and our homes were saved.' And the people bowed" (Exodus 12:27).

One of the participants asks:

מַצָּה זוֹ שֶׁאָנוּ אוֹכְלִים, עַל שׁוּם מָה?

What is the meaning of the matzah that we eat?

Hold the matzah and show it to the others:

עַל שׁוּם שֶׁלֹּא הִסְפִּיק בְּצֵקָם שֶׁל אֲבוֹתֵינוּ לְהַחֲמִיץ, עַד שֶׁנִּגְלָה עֲלֵיהֶם מֶלֶךְ מַלְכֵי הַמְּלָכִים, הַקָּדוֹשׁ בָּרוּךְ הוּא, וּגְאָלָם, שֶׁנֶּאֱמַר: וַיֹּאפוּ אֶת־הַבָּצֵק, אֲשֶׁר הוֹצִיאוּ מִמִּצְרַיִם, עֻגֹת מַצּוֹת, כִּי לֹא חָמֵץ. כִּי גֹרְשׁוּ מִמִּצְרַיִם, וְלֹא יָכְלוּ לְהִתְמַהְמֵהַּ, וְגַם צֵדָה לֹא עָשׂוּ לָהֶם.

This matzah is to remind us that before our ancestors' dough had time to rise, the Supreme Ruler, the Holy One, praised be God, revealed Himself to them and redeemed them. We read in the Torah, "They baked matzah out of the unleavened dough that they had brought out of Egypt; it did not rise because they were expelled from Egypt, and could not linger, nor had they prepared any food for the journey" (Exodus 12:39).

hope-giver

Matzah—Take 2

People have told me that getting stuck is one of the most serious reasons that they lose hope.

Being stuck in a habit, a relationship, or an attitude causes me to think I can never change.

At the beginning of the Seder we refer to matzah as "the bread of affliction that our forefathers ate in Egypt." We only see the negative side of matzah.

Toward the end of the haggadah, we describe matzah as the dough that didn't have time to rise as God was redeeming the Jewish People. The bread of affliction has now become the bread of liberation. Suddenly, the matzah is put into a larger context and everything changes.

The process of reframing an experience, of placing a negative moment into a larger context, is essential to our becoming unstuck.

What habit or relationship do you need to reframe, to de-stuckify?

53

One of the participants asks:

מָרוֹר זֶה שֶׁאָנוּ אוֹכְלִים, עַל שׁוּם מָה?

What is the meaning of the bitter herbs that we eat?

Hold the maror (bitter herb) and show it to the others.

עַל שׁוּם שֶׁמֵּרְרוּ הַמִּצְרִים אֶת־חַיֵּי אֲבוֹתֵינוּ בְּמִצְרָיִם, שֶׁנֶּאֱמַר: וַיְמָרֲרוּ אֶת־חַיֵּיהֶם בַּעֲבֹדָה קָשָׁה, בְּחֹמֶר וּבִלְבֵנִים, וּבְכָל־עֲבֹדָה בַּשָּׂדֶה. אֵת כָּל־עֲבֹדָתָם, אֲשֶׁר עָבְדוּ בָהֶם בְּפָרֶךְ.

This maror (bitter herb) is to remind us that the Egyptians embittered the lives of our ancestors in Egypt, as we learn in the Torah: "They made their lives bitter with hard labor, with mortar and brick, and with every kind of work in the field. All the labor that the Egyptians forced upon them was excessively harsh" (Exodus 1:14).

hope-giver

54

Maror

Bad times. Chewing on bad times.

In my family, we have a custom of biting into a big chunk of horseradish during the Seder. Faces turn red; eyes wince; we're burning from the inside.

And then it is over. A big "Aahhh." Each person takes a deep breath. We've survived maror.

The bitterness of maror is an essential part of the Seder. The Torah tells us that the Passover sacrifice should be eaten together with maror to remind us how the Egyptians embittered our lives with hard, mind-numbing work.

Slavery imprinted trauma on our souls that did not disappear when we crossed the Red Sea. Generations of anguish, physical and spiritual, do not just vanish. They linger in the inner recesses of our lives, waiting to be triggered. They can control us.

The bitterness of disempowerment and persecution is still with us, whether or not we choose to acknowledge it. We need to revisit the bitterness every year—to face it, taste it, own it, and conquer it.

With the exhaling of the "Aahhh" comes fresh hope of moving ahead. We will not let lingering bitterness paralyze or diminish us. We have confronted it head on, we have chewed on it once again and survived to tell our story.

What are the difficult moments in Jewish history that, looking back now, give you hope?

hope-giver

55

בְּכָל־דּוֹר וָדוֹר חַיָּב אָדָם לִרְאוֹת אֶת־עַצְמוֹ, כְּאִלּוּ הוּא יָצָא מִמִּצְרָיִם, שֶׁנֶּאֱמַר: וְהִגַּדְתָּ לְבִנְךָ בַּיּוֹם הַהוּא לֵאמֹר: בַּעֲבוּר זֶה עָשָׂה יְיָ לִי, בְּצֵאתִי מִמִּצְרָיִם. לֹא אֶת־אֲבוֹתֵינוּ בִּלְבָד גָּאַל הַקָּדוֹשׁ בָּרוּךְ הוּא, אֶלָּא אַף אוֹתָנוּ גָּאַל עִמָּהֶם, שֶׁנֶּאֱמַר: וְאוֹתָנוּ הוֹצִיא מִשָּׁם, לְמַעַן הָבִיא אֹתָנוּ, לָתֶת לָנוּ אֶת־הָאָרֶץ אֲשֶׁר נִשְׁבַּע לַאֲבֹתֵינוּ.

In every generation, each Jew should regard him/herself as having personally gone forth from Egypt. That is what the Torah means when it says, "And you should tell your son on that day, saying, 'It is because of what God did for me when I went forth from Egypt'" (Exodus 13:8). It was not only our ancestors whom the Holy One, praised be God, redeemed from slavery, but us as well, as we read, "God brought us out from there, in order to bring us to this land, and give us this land which was promised to our ancestors" (Deuteronomy 6:23).

seniors

What would you say was the greatest moment for the Jewish People in your lifetime?

56

Hold the cup, cover the matzah, and say:

לְפִיכָךְ אֲנַחְנוּ חַיָּבִים לְהוֹדוֹת, לְהַלֵּל, לְשַׁבֵּחַ, לְפָאֵר, לְרוֹמֵם, לְהַדֵּר, לְבָרֵךְ, לְעַלֵּה וּלְקַלֵּס, לְמִי שֶׁעָשָׂה לַאֲבוֹתֵינוּ וְלָנוּ אֶת־כָּל־הַנִּסִּים הָאֵלּוּ. הוֹצִיאָנוּ מֵעַבְדוּת לְחֵרוּת, מִיָּגוֹן לְשִׂמְחָה, וּמֵאֵבֶל לְיוֹם טוֹב, וּמֵאֲפֵלָה לְאוֹר גָּדוֹל, וּמִשִּׁעְבּוּד לִגְאֻלָּה. וְנֹאמַר לְפָנָיו שִׁירָה חֲדָשָׁה. הַלְלוּיָהּ.

הַלְלוּיָהּ. הַלְלוּ עַבְדֵי יְיָ. הַלְלוּ אֶת־שֵׁם יְיָ. יְהִי שֵׁם יְיָ מְבֹרָךְ מֵעַתָּה וְעַד עוֹלָם. מִמִּזְרַח שֶׁמֶשׁ עַד מְבוֹאוֹ. מְהֻלָּל שֵׁם יְיָ. רָם עַל־כָּל־גּוֹיִם יְיָ. עַל הַשָּׁמַיִם כְּבוֹדוֹ. מִי כַּיְיָ אֱלֹהֵינוּ. הַמַּגְבִּיהִי לָשָׁבֶת. הַמַּשְׁפִּילִי לִרְאוֹת בַּשָּׁמַיִם וּבָאָרֶץ. מְקִימִי מֵעָפָר דָּל. מֵאַשְׁפֹּת יָרִים אֶבְיוֹן. לְהוֹשִׁיבִי עִם־נְדִיבִים. עִם נְדִיבֵי עַמּוֹ. מוֹשִׁיבִי עֲקֶרֶת הַבַּיִת אֵם הַבָּנִים שְׂמֵחָה. הַלְלוּיָהּ.

בְּצֵאת יִשְׂרָאֵל מִמִּצְרָיִם, בֵּית יַעֲקֹב מֵעַם לֹעֵז. הָיְתָה יְהוּדָה לְקָדְשׁוֹ. יִשְׂרָאֵל מַמְשְׁלוֹתָיו. הַיָּם רָאָה וַיָּנֹס, הַיַּרְדֵּן יִסֹּב לְאָחוֹר. הֶהָרִים רָקְדוּ כְאֵילִים. גְּבָעוֹת כִּבְנֵי־צֹאן. מַה־לְּךָ הַיָּם כִּי תָנוּס. הַיַּרְדֵּן תִּסֹּב לְאָחוֹר. הֶהָרִים תִּרְקְדוּ כְאֵילִים. גְּבָעוֹת כִּבְנֵי־צֹאן. מִלִּפְנֵי אָדוֹן חוּלִי אָרֶץ. מִלִּפְנֵי אֱלוֹהַּ יַעֲקֹב. הַהֹפְכִי הַצּוּר אֲגַם־מָיִם. חַלָּמִישׁ לְמַעְיְנוֹ־מָיִם.

Therefore we should thank and praise, laud and glorify, exalt and honor, bless, extol, and acclaim God who performed all these miracles for our ancestors and for us. God brought us from slavery to freedom, from sorrow to joy, from mourning to festivity, from darkness to great light, and from servitude to redemption. Let us then sing before the Divine a new song: praise our God!

Halleluyah! Servants of God, praise the Name of God. May the Name of God be praised from now and forever. From where the sun rises in the East to where it sets in the West, the Name of God is to be praised. God is supreme above all nations, divine glory takes over the heavens. Who is like our God, who sits on high, yet who looks down to consider both heaven and earth? God raises up the poor out of the dust and lifts up the needy from the pits, to seat them together with nobles, with the nobles of His people. The all-powerful One makes the childless wife a happy mother of children. Halleluyah! (Psalm 113).

When Israel went forth from Egypt, the house of Jacob from a people of strange tongue, Judah became God's sanctuary and Israel became the divine kingdom. The Red Sea saw the events and fled, the river Jordan turned back on its heels. The mountains danced like rams, the hills like young lambs. What ails you, O Sea, that you are fleeing; O Jordan, that you turn back on your heels? You mountains, that you dance like rams; you hills, like young lambs? Tremble, O earth, at the presence of God, at the presence of the God of Jacob, who turns the rock into a pool of water, the flint into a flowing spring (Psalm 114).

Second Cup of Wine

Raise the cup until we reach "Redeemer of Israel."

בָּרוּךְ אַתָּה יְיָ, אֱלֹהֵינוּ מֶלֶךְ הָעוֹלָם, אֲשֶׁר גְּאָלָנוּ וְגָאַל אֶת־אֲבוֹתֵינוּ מִמִּצְרַיִם, וְהִגִּיעָנוּ לַלַּיְלָה הַזֶּה, לֶאֱכָל־בּוֹ מַצָּה וּמָרוֹר. כֵּן, יְיָ אֱלֹהֵינוּ וֵאלֹהֵי אֲבוֹתֵינוּ, יַגִּיעֵנוּ לְמוֹעֲדִים וְלִרְגָלִים אֲחֵרִים, הַבָּאִים לִקְרָאתֵנוּ לְשָׁלוֹם. שְׂמֵחִים בְּבִנְיַן עִירֶךָ, וְשָׂשִׂים בַּעֲבוֹדָתֶךָ, וְנֹאכַל שָׁם מִן הַזְּבָחִים וּמִן הַפְּסָחִים (on Saturday night say מִן הַפְּסָחִים וּמִן הַזְּבָחִים), אֲשֶׁר יַגִּיעַ דָּמָם, עַל קִיר מִזְבַּחֲךָ לְרָצוֹן, וְנוֹדֶה לְךָ שִׁיר חָדָשׁ עַל גְּאֻלָּתֵנוּ, וְעַל פְּדוּת נַפְשֵׁנוּ. בָּרוּךְ אַתָּה יְיָ, גָּאַל יִשְׂרָאֵל.

Praised are You, our God, Sovereign of the Universe, who redeemed us and redeemed our ancestors from Egypt, and enabled us to reach this night on which we eat matzah and maror (bitter herb). So too, our God, and God of our ancestors, please enable us to reach other holidays and festivals in peace, while rejoicing in the restoration of Your city Jerusalem and while finding delight in serving You. In the restored Jerusalem we will partake of the Passover offering and meal, bring You an offering that will be acceptable to You, and sing a new song of thanks and praise to You for our freedom and redemption. Praised are you, God, the past and future Redeemer of Israel.

Say the blessing below and drink the cup while reclining to the left.

הִנְנִי מוּכָן וּמְזֻמָּן לְקַיֵּם מִצְוַת לְקַיֵּם כּוֹס שֵׁנִי מֵאַרְבַּע כּוֹסוֹת לְשֵׁם יִחוּד קוּדְשָׁא בְּרִיךְ הוּא וּשְׁכִינְתֵּיהּ עַל־יְדֵי הַהוּא טָמִיר וְנֶעְלָם בְּשֵׁם כָּל־יִשְׂרָאֵל.

I am ready and willing to enact the precept of blessing this day over the second cup of wine. I do this to unite God's Presence and in the name of all of Israel.

בָּרוּךְ אַתָּה יְיָ, אֱלֹהֵינוּ מֶלֶךְ הָעוֹלָם, בּוֹרֵא פְּרִי הַגָּפֶן.

Praised are You, our God, Sovereign of the Universe, who creates the fruit of the vine.

Rachtzah ∘ רָחְצָה ∘ Washing Hands

Wash our hands and make the blessing:

בָּרוּךְ אַתָּה יְיָ אֱלֹהֵינוּ מֶלֶךְ הָעוֹלָם, אֲשֶׁר קִדְּשָׁנוּ בְּמִצְוֹתָיו, וְצִוָּנוּ עַל נְטִילַת יָדָיִם.

Praised are You, our God, Sovereign of the Universe, who has sanctified us with Your commandments and has given us the mitzvah of washing of the hands.

One should not speak until after making the next two blessings and eating the matzah.

Motzi Matzah ∘ מוֹצִיא מַצָּה ∘ Eating Matzah

Take the broken middle matzah in your hand between the two whole ones (upper and lower); hold the three pieces together and say the first blessing with the intention of eating from the top whole matzah, and then say the second blessing with the intention of eating from the middle broken matzah. Afterward, break off a piece from the top whole one and a piece from the broken one, dip them into salt, and eat both while reclining.

בָּרוּךְ אַתָּה יְיָ, אֱלֹהֵינוּ מֶלֶךְ הָעוֹלָם, הַמּוֹצִיא לֶחֶם מִן הָאָרֶץ.

Praised are You, our God, Sovereign of the Universe, who brings forth bread from the earth.

בָּרוּךְ אַתָּה יְיָ, אֱלֹהֵינוּ מֶלֶךְ הָעוֹלָם, אֲשֶׁר קִדְּשָׁנוּ בְּמִצְוֹתָיו וְצִוָּנוּ עַל אֲכִילַת מַצָּה.

Praised are You, our God, Sovereign of the Universe, who has sanctified us with Your commandments and given us the mitzvah of eating matzah.

Now break off a *kezayit* (the volume of one olive) of the two matzot held, and eat the two pieces together in reclining position.

Maror ∘ מָרוֹר ∘ The Bitter Herb

All present should take a piece of maror, dip into the charoset, shake off the charoset, make the blessing, and eat without reclining.

בָּרוּךְ אַתָּה יְיָ אֱלֹהֵינוּ מֶלֶךְ הָעוֹלָם, אֲשֶׁר קִדְּשָׁנוּ בְּמִצְוֹתָיו וְצִוָּנוּ עַל אֲכִילַת מָרוֹר.

Praised are You, our God, Sovereign of the Universe, who has sanctified us with Your commandments and given us the mitzvah of eating maror (bitter herb).

Now eat the maror, without reclining.

Korech ∘ כּוֹרֵךְ ∘ Mixing Bitter and Sweet

All present should take a piece from the third whole matzah with a piece of maror, wrap them together and eat them while reclining and without saying a blessing. Before eating it, say:

זֵכֶר לְמִקְדָּשׁ כְּהִלֵּל:

As a reminder of the Temple, we follow the practice of Hillel.

כֵּן עָשָׂה הִלֵּל בִּזְמַן שֶׁבֵּית הַמִּקְדָּשׁ הָיָה קַיָּם. הָיָה כּוֹרֵךְ פֶּסַח מַצָּה וּמָרוֹר וְאוֹכֵל בְּיַחַד. לְקַיֵּם מַה שֶׁנֶּאֱמַר: עַל־מַצּוֹת וּמְרֹרִים יֹאכְלֻהוּ.

This is what Hillel would do when the Temple existed: He would wrap the matzah with the maror (bitter herb) and eat them together, in order to fulfill what is taught in the Torah, "You should eat the paschal lamb with matzot and maror" (Exodus 12:8).

Now eat them together—in the reclining position.

one on one

Korech (Taking the matzah together with the bitter herb.)

How can you frame the bitterness into a necessary part of your journey? Looking back, what was a bitter experience that ended up being important for your personal journey and growth?

hope-giver

Love
Charoset—Everyone's Favorite

When the table is full of matzah, maror, a boiled egg, and lettuce, how could anyone not love the mixture of nuts, dates, cinnamon, apples, and wine? But it's not so easy to find the connection between charoset and Passover.

The ingredients of charoset are all mentioned in *Shir haShirim* (Song of Songs), the beautiful poem that many read at the end of the Seder. *Shir haShirim* can be interpreted as a vivid and sensual love song between two individuals and/or as a moving ballad between the Jewish People and God. Eating charoset is, in a sense, ingesting this love song, making it a biblical love potion. A spiritual aphrodisiac.

The face of someone who has fallen in love shines with hope.

Often, with the passing of years, the early spark felt when first falling in love fades. But when we look at old pictures and read the letters written in early romance, we can often rekindle the flames of our passion.

The Seder, with its four cups of wine, reclining posture, charoset, and lengthy discussion of the Jewish People's "first date" with God evokes and rekindles this love.

And as with all love stories, hope is renewed.

When was the first time you felt God's love for you? For the Jewish People?

61

Shulchan Orech · שֻׁלְחָן עוֹרֵךְ · Let's Eat

Now eat and drink to your heart's content. It is permitted to drink wine between the second and third cups.

Tzafun · צָפוּן · Afikoman

After the meal, all those present take a piece from the matzah that was hidden for the *afikoman*, and eat from it while reclining. Before eating the *afikoman*, say:

זֵכֶר לְקָרְבָּן פֶּסַח הַנֶּאֱכַל עַל הָשׂבַע.   In memory of the Passover sacrifice that was eaten upon being satiated.

Tzafun—Finding the Missing Piece

We're almost at the end of the Seder. We've learned a lot about each other and hopefully also about ourselves.

Tzafun means "hidden." We start the journey by hiding a piece of the matzah. There is always something missing—for us individually, for our family and community, and for the Jewish People as a whole. The journey continues and continues.

As you stop and reflect on this year's Seder, what piece did you find? What are your thoughts about this year's Seder? What gave you hope?

Barech ○ בָּרֵךְ ○ Blessing the Meal

Pour the third cup and recite the Blessing after the Meal.

שִׁיר הַמַּעֲלוֹת בְּשׁוּב יְיָ אֶת שִׁיבַת צִיּוֹן הָיִינוּ כְּחֹלְמִים. אָז יִמָּלֵא שְׂחוֹק פִּינוּ וּלְשׁוֹנֵנוּ רִנָּה אָז יֹאמְרוּ בַגּוֹיִם הִגְדִּיל יְיָ לַעֲשׂוֹת עִם אֵלֶּה. הִגְדִּיל יְיָ לַעֲשׂוֹת עִמָּנוּ הָיִינוּ שְׂמֵחִים. שׁוּבָה יְיָ אֶת שְׁבִיתֵנוּ כַּאֲפִיקִים בַּנֶּגֶב. הַזֹּרְעִים בְּדִמְעָה בְּרִנָּה יִקְצֹרוּ. הָלוֹךְ יֵלֵךְ וּבָכֹה נֹשֵׂא מֶשֶׁךְ הַזָּרַע בֹּא יָבֹא בְרִנָּה נֹשֵׂא אֲלֻמֹּתָיו.

"A Song of Ascents. When our God will bring back the exiles of Zion, we will be as in a dream. Then our mouths will fill with laughter and our tongues with joyous song. Then it will be said among the nations, "God has done great things for them." Yes, God has done great things for us, and we rejoice. God, bring back our exiles like streams in the desert. Those who sow with tears will reap in joy. The one who weeps while scattering seed will return with joyful song while carrying home the sheaves" (Psalm 126).

When three or more have eaten together, the following introduction to the *Birkat Hamazon* (Blessing the Meal) is added:

<div dir="rtl">רַבּוֹתַי נְבָרֵךְ!</div>	Leader	Let us say the blessing for our food.
<div dir="rtl">יְהִי שֵׁם יְיָ מְבֹרָךְ מֵעַתָּה וְעַד עוֹלָם.</div>	Participants	Praised be the Name of God from now and forever (Psalm 113:2).
<div dir="rtl">יְהִי שֵׁם יְיָ מְבֹרָךְ מֵעַתָּה וְעַד עוֹלָם. בִּרְשׁוּת מָרָנָן וְרַבָּנָן וְרַבּוֹתַי, נְבָרֵךְ (say with ten adults) אֱלֹהֵינוּ שֶׁאָכַלְנוּ מִשֶּׁלוֹ.</div>	Leader	Praised be the Name of God from now and forever (Psalm 113:2). With the permission of those present, let us bless the One (say with ten adults: our God) from whose bounty we have eaten.
<div dir="rtl">בָּרוּךְ (say with ten adults) אֱלֹהֵינוּ שֶׁאָכַלְנוּ מִשֶּׁלוֹ וּבְטוּבוֹ חָיִינוּ.</div>	Participants	Praised be the One (say with ten adults: our God) from whose bounty we have eaten and through whose goodness we live.
<div dir="rtl">בָּרוּךְ (say with ten adults) אֱלֹהֵינוּ שֶׁאָכַלְנוּ מִשֶּׁלוֹ וּבְטוּבוֹ חָיִינוּ.</div>	Leader	Praised be the One (say with ten adults: our God) from whose bounty we have eaten and through whose goodness we live.
<div dir="rtl">בָּרוּךְ הוּא וּבָרוּךְ שְׁמוֹ:</div>	All	Praised be the One.

בָּרוּךְ אַתָּה יְיָ, אֱלֹהֵינוּ מֶלֶךְ הָעוֹלָם, הַזָּן אֶת הָעוֹלָם כֻּלּוֹ בְּטוּבוֹ בְּחֵן בְּחֶסֶד וּבְרַחֲמִים הוּא נוֹתֵן לֶחֶם לְכָל בָּשָׂר כִּי לְעוֹלָם חַסְדּוֹ. וּבְטוּבוֹ הַגָּדוֹל תָּמִיד לֹא חָסַר לָנוּ, וְאַל יֶחְסַר לָנוּ מָזוֹן לְעוֹלָם וָעֶד. בַּעֲבוּר שְׁמוֹ הַגָּדוֹל, כִּי הוּא אֵל זָן וּמְפַרְנֵס לַכֹּל וּמֵטִיב לַכֹּל, וּמֵכִין מָזוֹן לְכֹל בְּרִיּוֹתָיו אֲשֶׁר בָּרָא. בָּרוּךְ אַתָּה יְיָ, הַזָּן אֶת הַכֹּל.

נוֹדֶה לְךָ יְיָ אֱלֹהֵינוּ עַל שֶׁהִנְחַלְתָּ לַאֲבוֹתֵינוּ, אֶרֶץ חֶמְדָּה טוֹבָה וּרְחָבָה, וְעַל שֶׁהוֹצֵאתָנוּ יְיָ אֱלֹהֵינוּ מֵאֶרֶץ מִצְרַיִם, וּפְדִיתָנוּ, מִבֵּית עֲבָדִים, וְעַל בְּרִיתְךָ שֶׁחָתַמְתָּ בִּבְשָׂרֵנוּ, וְעַל תּוֹרָתְךָ שֶׁלִּמַּדְתָּנוּ, וְעַל חֻקֶּיךָ שֶׁהוֹדַעְתָּנוּ וְעַל חַיִּים חֵן וָחֶסֶד שֶׁחוֹנַנְתָּנוּ, וְעַל אֲכִילַת מָזוֹן שָׁאַתָּה זָן וּמְפַרְנֵס אוֹתָנוּ תָּמִיד, בְּכָל יוֹם וּבְכָל עֵת וּבְכָל שָׁעָה.

וְעַל הַכֹּל יְיָ אֱלֹהֵינוּ אֲנַחְנוּ מוֹדִים לָךְ, וּמְבָרְכִים אוֹתָךְ, יִתְבָּרַךְ שִׁמְךָ בְּפִי כָּל חַי תָּמִיד לְעוֹלָם וָעֶד. כַּכָּתוּב, וְאָכַלְתָּ וְשָׂבָעְתָּ, וּבֵרַכְתָּ אֶת יְיָ אֱלֹהֶיךָ עַל הָאָרֶץ הַטֹּבָה אֲשֶׁר נָתַן לָךְ. בָּרוּךְ אַתָּה יְיָ, עַל הָאָרֶץ וְעַל הַמָּזוֹן.

רַחֵם נָא יְיָ אֱלֹהֵינוּ, עַל יִשְׂרָאֵל עַמֶּךָ, וְעַל יְרוּשָׁלַיִם עִירֶךָ, וְעַל צִיּוֹן מִשְׁכַּן כְּבוֹדֶךָ, וְעַל מַלְכוּת בֵּית דָּוִד מְשִׁיחֶךָ, וְעַל הַבַּיִת הַגָּדוֹל וְהַקָּדוֹשׁ שֶׁנִּקְרָא שִׁמְךָ עָלָיו. אֱלֹהֵינוּ, אָבִינוּ, רְעֵנוּ, זוּנֵנוּ, פַּרְנְסֵנוּ, וְכַלְכְּלֵנוּ, וְהַרְוִיחֵנוּ, וְהַרְוַח לָנוּ יְיָ אֱלֹהֵינוּ מְהֵרָה מִכָּל צָרוֹתֵינוּ, וְנָא, אַל תַּצְרִיכֵנוּ יְיָ אֱלֹהֵינוּ, לֹא לִידֵי מַתְּנַת בָּשָׂר וָדָם, וְלֹא לִידֵי הַלְוָאָתָם. כִּי אִם לְיָדְךָ הַמְּלֵאָה, הַפְּתוּחָה, הַקְּדוֹשָׁה וְהָרְחָבָה, שֶׁלֹּא נֵבוֹשׁ וְלֹא נִכָּלֵם לְעוֹלָם וָעֶד.

Praised are You, our God, Sovereign of the Universe, who sustains the entire world in Godly goodness, with grace, loving-kindness, and compassion. You provide food to all Your creatures since Your mercy is everlasting. Because of Your great goodness, we have not lacked sustenance. May we never lack sustenance for the sake of Your great Name. You, God, sustain all, do good for all, and provide food for all of Your creatures whom You have created. Praised are You, God, who provides food for all.

We thank you, our God, for the good, pleasant, and spacious land that You gave as an inheritance to our ancestors, for liberating us from the land of Egypt, and for redeeming us from the house of slaves. We thank You for the promise sealed in our flesh, for the Torah teaching that You impart to us, and for the limits of conduct that You made us know, and for life, for beauty, and for loving-kindness with which You are so generous. And we thank You for the joy of eating that You grant us while You nourish us, every day, every moment.

For all this, our God, we thank You and praise You; may Your Name be praised by every living being continually and forever. We do this to fulfill Your command, which states, "When you have eaten and you are satisfied, you shall praise your God for the earthy goodness that God so freely gave to you" (Deuteronomy 8:10). Praised are You, God, for the earth and for its produce.

Please remember in mercy, our God, Your people Israel; Your city Jerusalem; Zion, the dwelling place of Your glory; the heir to the throne of David, Your anointed one; and the great and holy house where it was so easy to call upon You. Our God, our Father, tend and nourish us, sustain and maintain us and please give us quick relief, our God, from all of our troubles. Permit us not to depend on gifts, handouts, or loans, our God, but may we only rely on Your full, open, and generous hand, so we never lose self-respect, nor suffer shame or disgrace.

64

On Shabbat say רְצֵה וְהַחֲלִיצֵנוּ יְיָ אֱלֹהֵינוּ בְּמִצְוֹתֶיךָ
וּבְמִצְוַת יוֹם הַשְּׁבִיעִי הַשַּׁבָּת הַגָּדוֹל וְהַקָּדוֹשׁ הַזֶּה. כִּי
יוֹם זֶה גָּדוֹל וְקָדוֹשׁ הוּא לְפָנֶיךָ, לִשְׁבָּת בּוֹ וְלָנוּחַ בּוֹ
בְּאַהֲבָה כְּמִצְוַת רְצוֹנֶךָ וּבִרְצוֹנְךָ הָנִיחַ לָנוּ יְיָ אֱלֹהֵינוּ,
שֶׁלֹּא תְהֵא צָרָה וְיָגוֹן וַאֲנָחָה בְּיוֹם מְנוּחָתֵנוּ. וְהַרְאֵנוּ יְיָ
אֱלֹהֵינוּ בְּנֶחָמַת צִיּוֹן עִירֶךָ, וּבְבִנְיַן יְרוּשָׁלַיִם עִיר קָדְשֶׁךָ,
כִּי אַתָּה הוּא בַּעַל הַיְשׁוּעוֹת וּבַעַל הַנֶּחָמוֹת.

אֱלֹהֵינוּ וֵאלֹהֵי אֲבוֹתֵינוּ, יַעֲלֶה וְיָבֹא וְיַגִּיעַ, וְיֵרָאֶה,
וְיֵרָצֶה, וְיִשָּׁמַע, וְיִפָּקֵד, וְיִזָּכֵר זִכְרוֹנֵנוּ וּפִקְדוֹנֵנוּ,
וְזִכְרוֹן אֲבוֹתֵינוּ, וְזִכְרוֹן מָשִׁיחַ בֶּן דָּוִד עַבְדֶּךָ, וְזִכְרוֹן
יְרוּשָׁלַיִם עִיר קָדְשֶׁךָ, וְזִכְרוֹן כָּל עַמְּךָ בֵּית יִשְׂרָאֵל
לְפָנֶיךָ, לִפְלֵיטָה לְטוֹבָה לְחֵן וּלְחֶסֶד וּלְרַחֲמִים, לְחַיִּים
וּלְשָׁלוֹם בְּיוֹם חַג הַמַּצּוֹת הַזֶּה. זָכְרֵנוּ יְיָ אֱלֹהֵינוּ בּוֹ
לְטוֹבָה. וּפָקְדֵנוּ בוֹ לִבְרָכָה. וְהוֹשִׁיעֵנוּ בוֹ לְחַיִּים, וּבִדְבַר
יְשׁוּעָה וְרַחֲמִים, חוּס וְחָנֵּנוּ, וְרַחֵם עָלֵינוּ וְהוֹשִׁיעֵנוּ, כִּי
אֵלֶיךָ עֵינֵינוּ, כִּי אֵל מֶלֶךְ חַנּוּן וְרַחוּם אָתָּה.

וּבְנֵה יְרוּשָׁלַיִם עִיר הַקֹּדֶשׁ בִּמְהֵרָה בְיָמֵינוּ. בָּרוּךְ אַתָּה
יְיָ, בּוֹנֵה בְרַחֲמָיו יְרוּשָׁלָיִם. אָמֵן.

On Shabbat, we add this paragraph, giving thanks for the Shabbat's rest:
Our God, strengthen us by Your commandments and especially by the commandment of the seventh day, this great and holy Shabbat. This day is great and holy before You, for in Your love You have given it as a day to rest, relax, and enjoy its peace, loving You all the more for the limits You set on our actions by Your will. On this day of rest, may there be no pain, no worry, no anguish, stress, or sighing. On this Shabbat day, open our eyes to the vision of the consolation of Zion and the building of Jerusalem, Your holy city, for You are at liberty to freely give liberation and consolation.

Our God and God of our ancestors, may this prayer we offer to You rise and come and reach You, be noted and accepted and heard by You, be remembered and acted upon, as You become aware of us and as You remember us. You remembered our parents; You will remember the Mashiach, David's son; You are mindful of Jerusalem, Your City; You are mindful of Israel, Your people. Allow them all to find their way to goodness, to grace, to loving-kindness, to mercy, to life, and to peace on this day of the Festival of Matzot. Remember us well on this day for life and well-being. And as concerns salvation and mercy, pity us, be kind, save us, be gentle, for we look to You, divine, majestic One, who is yet kind and gentle.

Rebuild Jerusalem, Your holy city, now and in our lifetime. Praised are You, who in building up mercy builds Jerusalem. Amen.

65

בָּרוּךְ אַתָּה יְיָ אֱלֹהֵינוּ מֶלֶךְ הָעוֹלָם, הָאֵל אָבִינוּ, מַלְכֵּנוּ, אַדִּירֵנוּ, בּוֹרְאֵנוּ, גּוֹאֲלֵנוּ, יוֹצְרֵנוּ, קְדוֹשֵׁנוּ קְדוֹשׁ יַעֲקֹב, רוֹעֵנוּ רוֹעֵה יִשְׂרָאֵל. הַמֶּלֶךְ הַטּוֹב, וְהַמֵּטִיב לַכֹּל, שֶׁבְּכָל יוֹם וָיוֹם הוּא הֵטִיב, הוּא מֵטִיב, הוּא יֵיטִיב לָנוּ. הוּא גְמָלָנוּ, הוּא גוֹמְלֵנוּ, הוּא יִגְמְלֵנוּ לָעַד, לְחֵן וּלְחֶסֶד וּלְרַחֲמִים וּלְרֶוַח הַצָּלָה וְהַצְלָחָה, בְּרָכָה וִישׁוּעָה, נֶחָמָה, פַּרְנָסָה וְכַלְכָּלָה, וְרַחֲמִים, וְחַיִּים וְשָׁלוֹם, וְכָל טוֹב, וּמִכָּל טוּב לְעוֹלָם אַל יְחַסְּרֵנוּ.

הָרַחֲמָן, הוּא יִמְלוֹךְ עָלֵינוּ לְעוֹלָם וָעֶד. הָרַחֲמָן, הוּא יִתְבָּרַךְ בַּשָּׁמַיִם וּבָאָרֶץ. הָרַחֲמָן, הוּא יִשְׁתַּבַּח לְדוֹר דּוֹרִים, וְיִתְפָּאַר בָּנוּ לָעַד וּלְנֵצַח נְצָחִים, וְיִתְהַדַּר בָּנוּ לָעַד וּלְעוֹלְמֵי עוֹלָמִים. הָרַחֲמָן, הוּא יְפַרְנְסֵנוּ בְּכָבוֹד. הָרַחֲמָן, הוּא יִשְׁבּוֹר עֻלֵּנוּ מֵעַל צַוָּארֵנוּ וְהוּא יוֹלִיכֵנוּ קוֹמְמִיּוּת לְאַרְצֵנוּ. הָרַחֲמָן, הוּא יִשְׁלַח לָנוּ בְּרָכָה מְרֻבָּה בַּבַּיִת הַזֶּה, וְעַל שֻׁלְחָן זֶה שֶׁאָכַלְנוּ עָלָיו. הָרַחֲמָן, הוּא יִשְׁלַח לָנוּ אֶת אֵלִיָּהוּ הַנָּבִיא זָכוּר לַטּוֹב, וִיבַשֶּׂר לָנוּ בְּשׂוֹרוֹת טוֹבוֹת יְשׁוּעוֹת וְנֶחָמוֹת.

הָרַחֲמָן, הוּא יְבָרֵךְ אֶת כָּל הַמְּסֻבִּין כַּאן, אוֹתָנוּ וְאֶת כָּל אֲשֶׁר לָנוּ, כְּמוֹ שֶׁנִּתְבָּרְכוּ אֲבוֹתֵינוּ, אַבְרָהָם יִצְחָק וְיַעֲקֹב בַּכֹּל, מִכֹּל, כֹּל, כֵּן יְבָרֵךְ אוֹתָנוּ כֻּלָּנוּ יַחַד בִּבְרָכָה שְׁלֵמָה, וְנֹאמַר אָמֵן.

Praised are You, our God, Sovereign of the Universe. You are God, our Parent, our Ruler, our Mighty One, our Creator, our Redeemer, our Maker, Jacob's Sanctifier, Guiding Shepherd, Israel's Shepherd, Sovereign who is good to all. You show us kindness day by day and You are good to us, and so may You deal with us in the future. As you have always bestowed Your bounty upon us, please continue to bless us freely and completely, kindly and mercifully, generously and abundantly, to save us, to prosper us, to bless us, to redeem us, to console us, to sustain and support us, in mercy, life, peace, and in goodness. Please never withhold Your goodness from us.

Compassionate One! Reign over us always. Compassionate One! May You be praised in the heavens and on earth. Compassionate One! You who are praised from one generation to the next, take pride in us always. May our lives honor You in this world and in the next. Compassionate One! Grant us an honorable livelihood. Compassionate One! End our oppression and lead the homeless of our people in dignity into our ancient homeland. Compassionate One! Send abundant blessing to this home and to this table. Compassionate One! Send Elijah the Prophet, of blessed memory, to bring good news of liberation and consolation. Compassionate One! Bless and protect all of us, our loved ones and our families, our endeavors and our possessions. May we all be blessed like our ancestors were blessed, with everything, by everyone and in every way. And to all this let us say, Amen!

Compassionate One. Please bless everyone here, us and all that is ours, just as our ancestors Abraham, Isaac, and Jacob were blessed with every blessing. So may God bless all of us together in a perfect blessing. And let us say: Amen.

66

בַּמָּרוֹם יְלַמְּדוּ עֲלֵיהֶם וְעָלֵינוּ זְכוּת, שֶׁתְּהֵא לְמִשְׁמֶרֶת שָׁלוֹם, וְנִשָּׂא בְרָכָה מֵאֵת יְיָ וּצְדָקָה מֵאֱלֹהֵי יִשְׁעֵנוּ, וְנִמְצָא חֵן וְשֵׂכֶל טוֹב בְּעֵינֵי אֱלֹהִים וְאָדָם.

On Shabbat say הָרַחֲמָן, הוּא יַנְחִילֵנוּ יוֹם שֶׁכֻּלּוֹ שַׁבָּת וּמְנוּחָה לְחַיֵּי הָעוֹלָמִים.

הָרַחֲמָן, הוּא יַנְחִילֵנוּ יוֹם שֶׁכֻּלּוֹ טוֹב. הָרַחֲמָן, הוּא יְזַכֵּנוּ לִימוֹת הַמָּשִׁיחַ וּלְחַיֵּי הָעוֹלָם הַבָּא.

מִגְדּוֹל יְשׁוּעוֹת מַלְכּוֹ, וְעֹשֶׂה חֶסֶד לִמְשִׁיחוֹ לְדָוִד וּלְזַרְעוֹ עַד עוֹלָם. עֹשֶׂה שָׁלוֹם בִּמְרוֹמָיו, הוּא יַעֲשֶׂה שָׁלוֹם, עָלֵינוּ וְעַל כָּל יִשְׂרָאֵל, וְאִמְרוּ אָמֵן.

יְראוּ אֶת יְיָ קְדֹשָׁיו, כִּי אֵין מַחְסוֹר לִירֵאָיו. כְּפִירִים רָשׁוּ וְרָעֵבוּ, וְדֹרְשֵׁי יְיָ לֹא יַחְסְרוּ כָל טוֹב. הוֹדוּ לַיְיָ כִּי טוֹב, כִּי לְעוֹלָם חַסְדּוֹ. פּוֹתֵחַ אֶת יָדֶךָ, וּמַשְׂבִּיעַ לְכָל חַי רָצוֹן. בָּרוּךְ הַגֶּבֶר אֲשֶׁר יִבְטַח בַּיְיָ, וְהָיָה יְיָ מִבְטַחוֹ. נַעַר הָיִיתִי גַּם זָקַנְתִּי וְלֹא רָאִיתִי צַדִּיק נֶעֱזָב, וְזַרְעוֹ מְבַקֶּשׁ לָחֶם. יְיָ עֹז לְעַמּוֹ יִתֵּן, יְיָ יְבָרֵךְ אֶת עַמּוֹ בַשָּׁלוֹם.

May our merit and the merit of our ancestors secure for all of us enduring blessing and peace. And even if we are not deemed worthy, our helping God, please grant us blessing as a kind favor on Your part. May we ever be found pleasant and wise by You, God, and by all our fellow human beings.

On Shabbat say Compassionate One! Please grant us the uninterrupted joy and serenity of Shabbat in this world and its parallel, rest in the world to come.

Compassionate One! Please grant that this holiday will be full of goodness. Compassionate One! May You find us worthy of the Messianic era and of the life to come.

"God is a tower of deliverance for the chosen [human] ruler; and shows kindness to his anointed one, to David and his descendants forever" (2 Samuel 22:51). The One who makes peace above, please will you make peace upon us and upon all of Israel? And say, Amen.

Fear our God, you who make God holy; if you fear only God, what will you lack? Those who are self-sufficient, like young lions, may starve in relying on their own strength. But those who seek only God shall not lack all that is good (Psalm 34:10–11). Give thanks to God who is so good, whose kindness is ever wise to the world (Psalm 118:1). You open Your hand and satisfy the will of all living things (Psalm 146:16). Blessed are they who trust in God, for God will always be their guarantor (Jeremiah 17:7). I was young, now I'm old, yet never saw a righteous person so forsaken that their child seeks bread (Psalm 37:25). God will surely give strength to our people. God will bless our people with peace (Psalm 29:11).

Third Cup of Wine

הִנְנִי מוּכָן וּמְזֻמָּן לְקַיֵּם מִצְוַת כּוֹס שְׁלִישִׁי מֵאַרְבַּע כּוֹסוֹת לְשֵׁם יִחוּד קֻדְשָׁא בְּרִיךְ הוּא וּשְׁכִינְתֵּיהּ עַל־יְדֵי הַהוּא טָמִיר וְנֶעְלָם בְּשֵׁם כָּל־יִשְׂרָאֵל.

בָּרוּךְ אַתָּה יְיָ, אֱלֹהֵינוּ מֶלֶךְ הָעוֹלָם, בּוֹרֵא פְּרִי הַגָּפֶן.

Drink while leaning to the left.

I am ready and willing to enact the precept of blessing this day over the third cup of wine. I do this to unite God's Presence and in the name of all of Israel.

Praised are You, our God, Sovereign of the Universe, who creates the fruit of the vine.

Pour Out Your Wrath

Pour the cup of Elijah and open the door.

שְׁפֹךְ חֲמָתְךָ אֶל־הַגּוֹיִם אֲשֶׁר לֹא יְדָעוּךָ וְעַל־מַמְלָכוֹת אֲשֶׁר בְּשִׁמְךָ לֹא קָרָאוּ. כִּי אָכַל אֶת־יַעֲקֹב. וְאֶת־נָוֵהוּ הֵשַׁמּוּ. שְׁפָךְ־עֲלֵיהֶם זַעְמֶךָ, וַחֲרוֹן אַפְּךָ יַשִּׂיגֵם. תִּרְדֹּף בְּאַף וְתַשְׁמִידֵם, מִתַּחַת שְׁמֵי יְיָ.

Pour Your wrath upon the nations who do not know You and upon the kingdoms that have not called Your Name, for they have consumed Jacob and laid waste his habitation (Psalm 79:6–7). Pour out Your fury upon them and let Your anger overtake them (Psalm 69:25). Pursue them in anger and destroy them from under the skies of the Almighty God (Lamentations 3:66).

hope-giver

Opening the Door for Elijah

Elijah lived centuries after the Exodus.

There is no connection between his actions and the Jews leaving Egypt. Yet he has become one of the central figures and symbols of the Passover Seder. Moses, the hero of the Exodus, is practically never mentioned. Yet we all know about Elijah's cup and opening the door for Elijah.

We pour the cup but do not drink it. We open the door but no one comes in.

The prophet Malachi says, "Behold, I will send you Elijah the prophet, before the coming of the great and awesome day of God. And he will turn the heart of fathers to their children and the heart of children to their fathers" (4:5–6).

Elijah brings together the hearts of people and generations. Elijah is the peacemaker in a world of strife and discord. Opening the door for Elijah is a harbinger of better times ahead.

The Seder is not about a single moment of redemption that occurred thousands of years ago. By remembering the Exodus from Egypt, we rekindle our hope in the ultimate breakthrough—however long it takes—to peace and harmony.

Elijah is the messenger of hope. Would we recognize Elijah if he were standing at the door when we opened it? Can a complete stranger actually bring us peace and hope in our lives?

Have you ever had an "Elijah the Prophet moment," when a complete stranger suddenly appeared and brought you peace and hope?

69

Hallel · הַלֵּל · Praising God

Pour the fourth cup of wine.

לֹא לָנוּ יְיָ לֹא לָנוּ כִּי לְשִׁמְךָ תֵּן כָּבוֹד, עַל חַסְדְּךָ,
עַל אֲמִתֶּךָ. לָמָּה יֹאמְרוּ הַגּוֹיִם, אַיֵּה נָא אֱלֹהֵיהֶם.
וֵאלֹהֵינוּ בַשָּׁמַיִם כֹּל אֲשֶׁר חָפֵץ עָשָׂה. עֲצַבֵּיהֶם
כֶּסֶף וְזָהָב, מַעֲשֵׂה יְדֵי אָדָם. פֶּה לָהֶם וְלֹא
יְדַבֵּרוּ, עֵינַיִם לָהֶם וְלֹא יִרְאוּ. אָזְנַיִם לָהֶם וְלֹא
יִשְׁמָעוּ, אַף לָהֶם וְלֹא יְרִיחוּן. יְדֵיהֶם וְלֹא יְמִישׁוּן,
רַגְלֵיהֶם וְלֹא יְהַלֵּכוּ, לֹא יֶהְגּוּ בִּגְרוֹנָם. כְּמוֹהֶם
יִהְיוּ עֹשֵׂיהֶם, כֹּל אֲשֶׁר בֹּטֵחַ בָּהֶם. יִשְׂרָאֵל בְּטַח
בַּייָ, עֶזְרָם וּמָגִנָּם הוּא. בֵּית אַהֲרֹן בִּטְחוּ בַייָ,
עֶזְרָם וּמָגִנָּם הוּא. יִרְאֵי יְיָ בִּטְחוּ בַייָ, עֶזְרָם
וּמָגִנָּם הוּא.

יְיָ זְכָרָנוּ יְבָרֵךְ, יְבָרֵךְ אֶת בֵּית יִשְׂרָאֵל, יְבָרֵךְ אֶת
בֵּית אַהֲרֹן. יְבָרֵךְ יִרְאֵי יְיָ, הַקְּטַנִּים עִם הַגְּדֹלִים.
יֹסֵף יְיָ עֲלֵיכֶם, עֲלֵיכֶם וְעַל בְּנֵיכֶם. בְּרוּכִים אַתֶּם
לַייָ, עֹשֵׂה שָׁמַיִם וָאָרֶץ. הַשָּׁמַיִם שָׁמַיִם לַייָ,
וְהָאָרֶץ נָתַן לִבְנֵי אָדָם. לֹא הַמֵּתִים יְהַלְלוּ יָהּ, וְלֹא
כָּל יֹרְדֵי דוּמָה. וַאֲנַחְנוּ נְבָרֵךְ יָהּ, מֵעַתָּה וְעַד
עוֹלָם, הַלְלוּיָהּ.

Not for us should You perform great acts and care for us, but rather to give glory to Your Name for Your kindness and for Your faithfulness. Why should the nations say, "Where is the Jewish People's God?" When in fact, our God is in heaven and has the ability to do anything. Their idols are silver and gold, the craft of human hands. Idols have mouths but cannot speak; they have eyes but cannot see. They have ears but cannot hear; they have noses but cannot smell. Their hands cannot feel. Their feet cannot walk. They cannot speak with their throats. The makers of idols, and those who trust in them, are likewise deceiving themselves that they can do these things. Israel trusts in its God, who is their helper and guardian. The family of Aaron trusts in its God; those who fear God, trust in God. God remembers us!

May God bless the family of Israel; may God bless the family of Aaron; may God bless those who fear God, whether they are small or great. May God shower abundance on you and your children. Welcomed and blessed are you by God, Maker of heaven and earth. Although the heavens are God's domain, the earth was given to humanity. The dead cannot praise God, nor can those who go retreat into silence. But we will praise God from now to eternity. Halleluyah! (Psalm 115).

אָהַבְתִּי כִּי יִשְׁמַע יְיָ אֶת קוֹלִי תַּחֲנוּנָי. כִּי הִטָּה אָזְנוֹ לִי וּבְיָמַי אֶקְרָא. אֲפָפוּנִי חֶבְלֵי מָוֶת, וּמְצָרֵי שְׁאוֹל מְצָאוּנִי. צָרָה וְיָגוֹן אֶמְצָא, וּבְשֵׁם יְיָ אֶקְרָא. אָנָּה יְיָ מַלְּטָה נַפְשִׁי. חַנּוּן יְיָ וְצַדִּיק, וֵאלֹהֵינוּ מְרַחֵם. שֹׁמֵר פְּתָאיִם יְיָ דַּלּוֹתִי וְלִי יְהוֹשִׁיעַ. שׁוּבִי נַפְשִׁי לִמְנוּחָיְכִי, כִּי יְיָ גָּמַל עָלָיְכִי. כִּי חִלַּצְתָּ נַפְשִׁי מִמָּוֶת אֶת עֵינִי מִן דִּמְעָה, אֶת רַגְלִי מִדֶּחִי. אֶתְהַלֵּךְ לִפְנֵי יְיָ, בְּאַרְצוֹת הַחַיִּים. הֶאֱמַנְתִּי כִּי אֲדַבֵּר, אֲנִי עָנִיתִי מְאֹד. אֲנִי אָמַרְתִּי בְחָפְזִי כָּל הָאָדָם כֹּזֵב.

מָה אָשִׁיב לַיְיָ, כָּל תַּגְמוּלוֹהִי עָלָי. כּוֹס יְשׁוּעוֹת אֶשָּׂא, וּבְשֵׁם יְיָ אֶקְרָא. נְדָרַי לַיְיָ אֲשַׁלֵּם, נֶגְדָה נָּא לְכָל עַמּוֹ. יָקָר בְּעֵינֵי יְיָ הַמָּוְתָה לַחֲסִידָיו. אָנָּה יְיָ כִּי אֲנִי עַבְדֶּךָ אֲנִי עַבְדְּךָ, בֶּן אֲמָתֶךָ פִּתַּחְתָּ לְמוֹסֵרָי. לְךָ אֶזְבַּח זֶבַח תּוֹדָה וּבְשֵׁם יְיָ אֶקְרָא. נְדָרַי לַיְיָ אֲשַׁלֵּם נֶגְדָה נָּא לְכָל עַמּוֹ. בְּחַצְרוֹת בֵּית יְיָ בְּתוֹכֵכִי יְרוּשָׁלָיִם הַלְלוּיָהּ.

הַלְלוּ אֶת יְיָ, כָּל גּוֹיִם, שַׁבְּחוּהוּ כָּל הָאֻמִּים. כִּי גָבַר עָלֵינוּ חַסְדּוֹ, וֶאֱמֶת יְיָ לְעוֹלָם הַלְלוּיָהּ.

הוֹדוּ לַיְיָ כִּי טוֹב, כִּי לְעוֹלָם חַסְדּוֹ:

יֹאמַר נָא יִשְׂרָאֵל, כִּי לְעוֹלָם חַסְדּוֹ:

יֹאמְרוּ נָא בֵית אַהֲרֹן, כִּי לְעוֹלָם חַסְדּוֹ:

יֹאמְרוּ נָא יִרְאֵי יְיָ, כִּי לְעוֹלָם חַסְדּוֹ:

I love that God hears my voice and my supplication. Since God turned an ear to me, I have cried out to God throughout my life. The ropes of death entangled me; the afflictions of the underworld came upon me; I found only pain and strife. I called out to God, "Please, God, save my life!" Our God is kind and just, our God demonstrates mercy. Our God protects the simple; I was brought low and God saved me. Be at rest again, my soul, for God has heaped good upon me. You have delivered me from death, my eyes from tears, my feet from stumbling. I will walk before God in the land of the living! All this because I had faith even when I said, "I am in great despair;" [even when] I said rashly, "All humans are deceitful" (Psalm 116:1–11).

How can I repay God for all the kindness that has been bestowed upon me? I raise the cup of deliverance and call out to honor the Name of God. I will fulfill my vow to God, truly, in the presence of all God's people. God does not regard the death of those who love God lightly. I beseech You, God, for I am Your servant, child of Your servant, and You have opened my chains. I will give a thanksgiving offering to You and call upon God by name. I will fulfill my vow to God, truly, in the presence of all God's people, in the courtyards of the house of God, in your midst, Jerusalem. Halleluyah! (Psalm 116:12–19).

Praise God, all you nations. Extol God, all you peoples! For God's love is great upon all people, and the truth of God is eternal. Halleluyah!

Give thanks to God, for God is good. God's kindness endures forever.

Israel, let us now say, "God's kindness endures forever."

Let the house of Aaron say, "God's kindness endures forever."

Let those who revere God say, "God's kindness endures forever" (Psalm 117–118:4).

מִן הַמֵּצַר קָרָאתִי יָּה, עֲנָנִי בַמֶּרְחָב יָהּ. יְיָ לִי לֹא אִירָא, מַה יַּעֲשֶׂה לִי אָדָם. יְיָ לִי בְּעֹזְרָי, וַאֲנִי אֶרְאֶה בְשֹׂנְאָי. טוֹב לַחֲסוֹת בַּיְיָ, מִבְּטֹחַ בָּאָדָם. טוֹב לַחֲסוֹת בַּיְיָ מִבְּטֹחַ בִּנְדִיבִים. כָּל גּוֹיִם סְבָבוּנִי בְּשֵׁם יְיָ כִּי אֲמִילַם. סַבּוּנִי גַם סְבָבוּנִי בְּשֵׁם יְיָ כִּי אֲמִילַם. סַבּוּנִי כִדְבֹרִים דֹּעֲכוּ כְּאֵשׁ קוֹצִים, בְּשֵׁם יְיָ כִּי אֲמִילַם. דָּחֹה דְחִיתַנִי לִנְפֹּל, וַיְיָ עֲזָרָנִי. עָזִּי וְזִמְרָת יָהּ, וַיְהִי לִי לִישׁוּעָה.

I have called upon God from my lowest place; God answered me with great generosity. God is at my side, so I do not fear anything that mortals can do to me. God is for me as my aid; I can look with calmness at those who hate me. Better to trust in God than trust in humans; better to trust in God than trust in nobles or powerful people. All the nations surround me, but by God's Name I will endure them. They surround me, they encompass me, but by God's Name I will endure them. They swarm around me like bees, they wither me down as fire to a thorn bush, but by God's Name I will endure them. I felt pushed off balance, about to fall, but God helped me stand straight and tall. God is my strength and song; God has become my deliverance.

קוֹל רִנָּה וִישׁוּעָה בְּאָהֳלֵי צַדִּיקִים, יְמִין יְיָ עֹשָׂה חָיִל. יְמִין יְיָ רוֹמֵמָה, יְמִין יְיָ עֹשָׂה חָיִל. לֹא אָמוּת כִּי אֶחְיֶה, וַאֲסַפֵּר מַעֲשֵׂי יָהּ. יַסֹּר יִסְּרַנִּי יָּהּ, וְלַמָּוֶת לֹא נְתָנָנִי. פִּתְחוּ לִי שַׁעֲרֵי צֶדֶק, אָבֹא בָם אוֹדֶה יָהּ. זֶה הַשַּׁעַר לַיְיָ, צַדִּיקִים יָבֹאוּ בוֹ.

The sound of happy song and salvation fills the tents of the righteous. Your hand, God, does mighty deeds. I will not die but I will live—and declare the works of God. God has chastised me greatly, but has not given me over to death. Open for me the gates of righteousness; I will enter them and praise God. This is the gate of God; let the righteous enter (Psalm 118:5–20).

אוֹדְךָ כִּי עֲנִיתָנִי, וַתְּהִי לִי לִישׁוּעָה. אוֹדְךָ כִּי עֲנִיתָנִי וַתְּהִי לִי לִישׁוּעָה. אֶבֶן מָאֲסוּ הַבּוֹנִים, הָיְתָה לְרֹאשׁ פִּנָּה. אֶבֶן מָאֲסוּ הַבּוֹנִים, הָיְתָה לְרֹאשׁ פִּנָּה. מֵאֵת יְיָ הָיְתָה זֹּאת, הִיא נִפְלָאת בְּעֵינֵינוּ. מֵאֵת יְיָ הָיְתָה זֹּאת, הִיא נִפְלָאת בְּעֵינֵינוּ. זֶה הַיּוֹם עָשָׂה יְיָ, נָגִילָה וְנִשְׂמְחָה בוֹ. זֶה הַיּוֹם עָשָׂה יְיָ נָגִילָה וְנִשְׂמְחָה בוֹ.

I will thank You, since You answered me, and You have been my deliverance. The stone that the builders rejected has become the main cornerstone. This is God's doing; it is wondrous to us. This is the day that God has made; let us rejoice and celebrate on it (Psalm 118:21–24).

אָנָּא יְיָ הוֹשִׁיעָה נָּא:

Please, God, deliver us now!

אָנָּא יְיָ הוֹשִׁיעָה נָּא:

Please, God, deliver us now!

אָנָּא יְיָ הַצְלִיחָה נָא:

Please, God, grant us success now!

אָנָּא יְיָ הַצְלִיחָה נָא:

Please, God, grant us success now! (Psalm 118:25).

THE AYEKA HAGGADAH

בָּרוּךְ הַבָּא בְּשֵׁם יְיָ, בֵּרַכְנוּכֶם מִבֵּית יְיָ. בָּרוּךְ הַבָּא בְּשֵׁם יְיָ, בֵּרַכְנוּכֶם מִבֵּית יְיָ. אֵל יְיָ וַיָּאֶר לָנוּ, אִסְרוּ חַג בַּעֲבֹתִים עַד קַרְנוֹת הַמִּזְבֵּחַ. אֵל יְיָ וַיָּאֶר לָנוּ, אִסְרוּ חַג בַּעֲבֹתִים, עַד קַרְנוֹת הַמִּזְבֵּחַ. אֵלִי אַתָּה וְאוֹדֶךָּ אֱלֹהַי אֲרוֹמְמֶךָּ. אֵלִי אַתָּה וְאוֹדֶךָּ אֱלֹהַי אֲרוֹמְמֶךָּ. הוֹדוּ לַיְיָ כִּי טוֹב, כִּי לְעוֹלָם חַסְדּוֹ. הוֹדוּ לַיְיָ כִּי טוֹב, כִּי לְעוֹלָם חַסְדּוֹ.

הוֹדוּ לַיְיָ כִּי טוֹב, כִּי לְעוֹלָם חַסְדּוֹ. הוֹדוּ לֵאלֹהֵי הָאֱלֹהִים, כִּי לְעוֹלָם חַסְדּוֹ. הוֹדוּ לַאֲדֹנֵי הָאֲדֹנִים, כִּי לְעוֹלָם חַסְדּוֹ. לְעֹשֵׂה נִפְלָאוֹת גְּדֹלוֹת לְבַדּוֹ, כִּי לְעוֹלָם חַסְדּוֹ. לְעֹשֵׂה הַשָּׁמַיִם בִּתְבוּנָה, כִּי לְעוֹלָם חַסְדּוֹ. לְרוֹקַע הָאָרֶץ עַל הַמָּיִם, כִּי לְעוֹלָם חַסְדּוֹ. לְעֹשֵׂה אוֹרִים גְּדֹלִים, כִּי לְעוֹלָם חַסְדּוֹ. אֶת הַשֶּׁמֶשׁ לְמֶמְשֶׁלֶת בַּיּוֹם, כִּי לְעוֹלָם חַסְדּוֹ. אֶת הַיָּרֵחַ וְכוֹכָבִים לְמֶמְשְׁלוֹת בַּלָּיְלָה, כִּי לְעוֹלָם חַסְדּוֹ. לְמַכֵּה מִצְרַיִם בִּבְכוֹרֵיהֶם, כִּי לְעוֹלָם חַסְדּוֹ. וַיּוֹצֵא יִשְׂרָאֵל מִתּוֹכָם, כִּי לְעוֹלָם חַסְדּוֹ. בְּיָד חֲזָקָה וּבִזְרוֹעַ נְטוּיָה, כִּי לְעוֹלָם חַסְדּוֹ. לְגֹזֵר יַם סוּף לִגְזָרִים, כִּי לְעוֹלָם חַסְדּוֹ. וְהֶעֱבִיר יִשְׂרָאֵל בְּתוֹכוֹ, כִּי לְעוֹלָם חַסְדּוֹ. וְנִעֵר פַּרְעֹה וְחֵילוֹ בְיַם סוּף, כִּי לְעוֹלָם חַסְדּוֹ. לְמוֹלִיךְ עַמּוֹ בַּמִּדְבָּר, כִּי לְעוֹלָם חַסְדּוֹ. לְמַכֵּה מְלָכִים גְּדֹלִים, כִּי לְעוֹלָם חַסְדּוֹ. וַיַּהֲרֹג מְלָכִים אַדִּירִים, כִּי לְעוֹלָם חַסְדּוֹ. לְסִיחוֹן מֶלֶךְ הָאֱמֹרִי, כִּי לְעוֹלָם חַסְדּוֹ. וּלְעוֹג מֶלֶךְ הַבָּשָׁן, כִּי לְעוֹלָם חַסְדּוֹ. וְנָתַן אַרְצָם לְנַחֲלָה, כִּי לְעוֹלָם חַסְדּוֹ. נַחֲלָה לְיִשְׂרָאֵל עַבְדּוֹ, כִּי לְעוֹלָם חַסְדּוֹ. שֶׁבְּשִׁפְלֵנוּ זָכַר לָנוּ, כִּי לְעוֹלָם חַסְדּוֹ. וַיִּפְרְקֵנוּ מִצָּרֵינוּ, כִּי לְעוֹלָם חַסְדּוֹ. נֹתֵן לֶחֶם לְכָל בָּשָׂר, כִּי לְעוֹלָם חַסְדּוֹ. הוֹדוּ לְאֵל הַשָּׁמָיִם, כִּי לְעוֹלָם חַסְדּוֹ.

Blessed is the person who comes in God's Name: we bless you from the House of God. God is divine and has given us light; order the festival procession of branches until the edges of the altar! You are my God and I will thank You; my God, I will exalt You. Give thanks to God, for divine goodness, since God's kindness is forever (Psalm 118:26–29).

All of your creatures will praise You, our God. Your pious ones, the righteous who do Your will, and all of Your people Israel, will jubilantly thank, praise, extol, and glorify, and exalt and acclaim, and sanctify and coronate Your Name, our God. For to You it is good to give thanks, and about Your Name it is pleasant to sing, for you are God, forever and ever. Hallel, Songs of Praise and Thanks Praise God, for God is good! Praise the God of Gods, praise the Sovereign of Sovereigns. God creates great wonders alone. God makes the skies with wisdom. God sets the earth on its foundation. God makes great lights: the sun to rule by day; the moon and stars to rule by night. God smote the firstborn of Egypt, and took Israel from their midst, by a strong hand and an outstretched arm. God split the Sea of Reeds in two parts, and guided Israel through its waves, and cast Pharaoh and his army in the Sea, and led the people in the wilderness. God struck mighty kings, and smote powerful tyrants: Sichon king of the Amorites, and Og king of Bashan. God gave their land as a legacy to God's people Israel. God remembered us in our low times, and unshackled us from our enemies. God grants food to all flesh. Praise the God of heaven—for God's kindness endures forever! (Psalm 136).

נִשְׁמַת כָּל חַי, תְּבָרֵךְ אֶת שִׁמְךָ יְיָ אֱלֹהֵינוּ. וְרוּחַ כָּל בָּשָׂר, תְּפָאֵר וּתְרוֹמֵם זִכְרְךָ מַלְכֵּנוּ תָּמִיד, מִן הָעוֹלָם וְעַד הָעוֹלָם אַתָּה אֵל. וּמִבַּלְעָדֶיךָ אֵין לָנוּ מֶלֶךְ גּוֹאֵל וּמוֹשִׁיעַ, פּוֹדֶה וּמַצִּיל וּמְפַרְנֵס וּמְרַחֵם, בְּכָל עֵת צָרָה וְצוּקָה. אֵין לָנוּ מֶלֶךְ אֶלָּא אָתָּה. אֱלֹהֵי הָרִאשׁוֹנִים וְהָאַחֲרוֹנִים, אֱלוֹהַּ כָּל בְּרִיּוֹת, אֲדוֹן כָּל תּוֹלָדוֹת, הַמְהֻלָּל בְּרֹב הַתִּשְׁבָּחוֹת, הַמְנַהֵג עוֹלָמוֹ בְּחֶסֶד, וּבְרִיּוֹתָיו בְּרַחֲמִים. וַיְיָ לֹא יָנוּם וְלֹא יִישָׁן, הַמְעוֹרֵר יְשֵׁנִים וְהַמֵּקִיץ נִרְדָּמִים, וְהַמֵּשִׂיחַ אִלְּמִים, וְהַמַּתִּיר אֲסוּרִים, וְהַסּוֹמֵךְ נוֹפְלִים, וְהַזּוֹקֵף כְּפוּפִים, לְךָ לְבַדְּךָ אֲנַחְנוּ מוֹדִים.

אִלּוּ פִינוּ מָלֵא שִׁירָה כַּיָּם, וּלְשׁוֹנֵנוּ רִנָּה כַּהֲמוֹן גַּלָּיו, וְשִׂפְתוֹתֵינוּ שֶׁבַח כְּמֶרְחֲבֵי רָקִיעַ, וְעֵינֵינוּ מְאִירוֹת כַּשֶּׁמֶשׁ וְכַיָּרֵחַ, וְיָדֵינוּ פְרוּשׂוֹת כְּנִשְׁרֵי שָׁמָיִם, וְרַגְלֵינוּ קַלּוֹת כָּאַיָּלוֹת, אֵין אֲנַחְנוּ מַסְפִּיקִים, לְהוֹדוֹת לְךָ יְיָ אֱלֹהֵינוּ וֵאלֹהֵי אֲבוֹתֵינוּ, וּלְבָרֵךְ אֶת שִׁמְךָ עַל אַחַת מֵאֶלֶף אֶלֶף אַלְפֵי אֲלָפִים וְרִבֵּי רְבָבוֹת פְּעָמִים, הַטּוֹבוֹת שֶׁעָשִׂיתָ עִם אֲבוֹתֵינוּ וְעִמָּנוּ.

מִמִּצְרַיִם גְּאַלְתָּנוּ יְיָ אֱלֹהֵינוּ, וּמִבֵּית עֲבָדִים פְּדִיתָנוּ, בְּרָעָב זַנְתָּנוּ, וּבְשָׂבָע כִּלְכַּלְתָּנוּ, מֵחֶרֶב הִצַּלְתָּנוּ, וּמִדֶּבֶר מִלַּטְתָּנוּ, וּמֵחֳלָיִם רָעִים וְנֶאֱמָנִים דִּלִּיתָנוּ. עַד הֵנָּה עֲזָרוּנוּ רַחֲמֶיךָ, וְלֹא עֲזָבוּנוּ חֲסָדֶיךָ וְאַל תִּטְּשֵׁנוּ יְיָ אֱלֹהֵינוּ לָנֶצַח.

The soul of every living being will praise Your Name, our God; the spirit moving in all flesh will make You glorious forever. From this world to the next, You are God, and without You we have no one else, no other redeemer, no other salvation. You set us free, You save us for life and sustain us. You answer us with compassion in times of anguish or distress. We have no one who helps us or nourishes us in the way that You do. God of the first and the last, God of all creatures and all generations, You are the One who is blessed in every song of praise. You infuse the world with kindness and show mercy to the life You have created. God is awake: God does not rest, nor does God sleep, but awakens those lost in slumber, stirs those who wander in dreams. God gives speech to the silent, seeks freedom for those who are imprisoned. God supports the fallen and raises up those who are bowed low; God unravels deep mysteries. To God alone we give thanks.

If our mouths were as full of song as is the sea and our speech as full of exultation as the roar of the waves, if our lips could utter as much praise as the wide-open spaces of heaven and our eyes sparkling like the sun and the moon, even if our hands could reach out to You like the eagle's wings spread out to the sky and our feet could run to You as swift as the deer, it would still not be nearly enough to thank You, our God and God of our ancestors, or to praise Your Name for even one thousandth of the thousands and thousands of miracles and wonders that You have given to our ancestors and to us.

You brought us safely out of Egypt, redeemed us from the house of slavery. You nourished us through famine and supported us with abundance. You rescued us from the sword, delivered us from plagues, and brought us through terrible sicknesses. Until now Your mercy has sustained us and Your kindness has never failed us; O God, do not ever abandon us.

74

עַל כֵּן אֲבָרִים שֶׁפִּלַּגְתָּ בָּנוּ, וְרוּחַ וּנְשָׁמָה שֶׁנָּפַחְתָּ בְּאַפֵּינוּ, וְלָשׁוֹן אֲשֶׁר שַׂמְתָּ בְּפִינוּ, הֵן הֵם יוֹדוּ וִיבָרְכוּ וִישַׁבְּחוּ וִיפָאֲרוּ וִירוֹמְמוּ וְיַעֲרִיצוּ וְיַקְדִּישׁוּ וְיַמְלִיכוּ אֶת שִׁמְךָ מַלְכֵּנוּ, כִּי כָל פֶּה לְךָ יוֹדֶה, וְכָל לָשׁוֹן לְךָ תִשָּׁבַע, וְכָל בֶּרֶךְ לְךָ תִכְרַע, וְכָל קוֹמָה לְפָנֶיךָ תִשְׁתַּחֲוֶה, וְכָל לְבָבוֹת יִירָאוּךָ, וְכָל קֶרֶב וּכְלָיוֹת יְזַמְּרוּ לִשְׁמֶךָ. כַּדָּבָר שֶׁכָּתוּב, כָּל עַצְמוֹתַי תֹּאמַרְנָה יְיָ מִי כָמוֹךָ. מַצִּיל עָנִי מֵחָזָק מִמֶּנּוּ, וְעָנִי וְאֶבְיוֹן מִגֹּזְלוֹ.

מִי יִדְמֶה לָּךְ, וּמִי יִשְׁוֶה לָּךְ וּמִי יַעֲרָךְ לָךְ. הָאֵל הַגָּדוֹל הַגִּבּוֹר וְהַנּוֹרָא, אֵל עֶלְיוֹן קֹנֵה שָׁמַיִם וָאָרֶץ. נְהַלֶּלְךָ וּנְשַׁבֵּחֲךָ וּנְפָאֶרְךָ וּנְבָרֵךְ אֶת־שֵׁם קָדְשֶׁךָ. כָּאָמוּר, לְדָוִד, בָּרְכִי נַפְשִׁי אֶת יְיָ, וְכָל קְרָבַי אֶת שֵׁם קָדְשׁוֹ.

הָאֵל בְּתַעֲצֻמוֹת עֻזֶּךָ, הַגָּדוֹל בִּכְבוֹד שְׁמֶךָ. הַגִּבּוֹר לָנֶצַח וְהַנּוֹרָא בְּנוֹרְאוֹתֶיךָ. הַמֶּלֶךְ הַיּוֹשֵׁב עַל כִּסֵּא רָם וְנִשָּׂא.

שׁוֹכֵן עַד, מָרוֹם וְקָדוֹשׁ שְׁמוֹ. וְכָתוּב, רַנְּנוּ צַדִּיקִים בַּיְיָ, לַיְשָׁרִים נָאוָה תְהִלָּה. בְּפִי יְשָׁרִים תִּתְהַלָּל. וּבְדִבְרֵי צַדִּיקִים תִּתְבָּרַךְ. וּבִלְשׁוֹן חֲסִידִים תִּתְרוֹמָם. וּבְקֶרֶב קְדוֹשִׁים תִּתְקַדָּשׁ.

Therefore, the limbs that You have given us, the breath and the soul that You have breathed into us, the language that You have put into our mouths, all these they thank You, praise, acclaim, and glorify You. They sing out to You, exalt and adore You, and sanctify Your Name, our Source. Every mouth acknowledges You, every tongue speaks to You with faith; every eye looks for You. Every knee will bend to You, and all who stand upright will bow down. All our hearts will seek You with reverence, even the vital organs inside us will praise Your Name, as it is written, "All my bones will say, who is like You, O God?" (Psalm 35:10). You save the poor from the oppressor and the helpless from the thieves who would prey upon them. You hear the cry of the weak; You listen and heed their plea for help.

Who is like You and who could be equal to You? Who could possibly compare with You, O God, powerful and exalted, Creator of heaven and earth? We will praise and glorify You, and will bless Your Holy Name, saying, "Bless God, O my soul; let everything that is in me bless God's Holy Name."

God, powerful in strength and magnificent in the glory of Your Name, heroic in endurance, revered for breathtaking wonders, Your Presence is enthroned, lofty, and eminent.

Dwelling in transcendent places, Your Name is exalted, Your Name is holy. The righteous sing joyfully to God; the just find beauty in prayer. In the mouths of the just You are exalted, on the lips of the righteous You are blessed, in the words of the faithful You are sanctified, and amongst the holy ones, You are praised.

וּבְמַקְהֲלוֹת רִבְבוֹת עַמְּךָ בֵּית יִשְׂרָאֵל, בְּרִנָּה יִתְפָּאַר שִׁמְךָ
מַלְכֵּנוּ, בְּכָל דּוֹר וָדוֹר, שֶׁכֵּן חוֹבַת כָּל הַיְצוּרִים, לְפָנֶיךָ יְיָ
אֱלֹהֵינוּ וֵאלֹהֵי אֲבוֹתֵינוּ, לְהוֹדוֹת לְהַלֵּל לְשַׁבֵּחַ לְפָאֵר לְרוֹמֵם
לְהַדֵּר לְבָרֵךְ לְעַלֵּה וּלְקַלֵּס, עַל כָּל דִּבְרֵי שִׁירוֹת וְתִשְׁבְּחוֹת
דָּוִד בֶּן יִשַׁי עַבְדְּךָ מְשִׁיחֶךָ.

יִשְׁתַּבַּח שִׁמְךָ לָעַד מַלְכֵּנוּ, הָאֵל הַמֶּלֶךְ הַגָּדוֹל וְהַקָּדוֹשׁ
בַּשָּׁמַיִם וּבָאָרֶץ. כִּי לְךָ נָאֶה, יְיָ אֱלֹהֵינוּ וֵאלֹהֵי אֲבוֹתֵינוּ. שִׁיר
וּשְׁבָחָה, הַלֵּל וְזִמְרָה, עֹז וּמֶמְשָׁלָה, נֶצַח, גְּדֻלָּה וּגְבוּרָה,
תְּהִלָּה וְתִפְאֶרֶת, קְדֻשָּׁה וּמַלְכוּת. בְּרָכוֹת וְהוֹדָאוֹת מֵעַתָּה
וְעַד עוֹלָם.

יְהַלְלוּךָ יְיָ אֱלֹהֵינוּ כָּל מַעֲשֶׂיךָ, וַחֲסִידֶיךָ צַדִּיקִים עוֹשֵׂי
רְצוֹנֶךָ, וְכָל עַמְּךָ בֵּית יִשְׂרָאֵל בְּרִנָּה יוֹדוּ וִיבָרְכוּ וִישַׁבְּחוּ
וִיפָאֲרוּ וִירוֹמְמוּ וְיַעֲרִיצוּ וְיַקְדִּישׁוּ וְיַמְלִיכוּ אֶת שִׁמְךָ מַלְכֵּנוּ,
כִּי לְךָ טוֹב לְהוֹדוֹת וּלְשִׁמְךָ נָאֶה לְזַמֵּר, כִּי מֵעוֹלָם וְעַד עוֹלָם
אַתָּה אֵל. בָּרוּךְ אַתָּה יְיָ, מֶלֶךְ מְהֻלָּל בַּתִּשְׁבָּחוֹת.

In the assemblies and the multitudes of Your people, Israel, Your Name will be praised with joy, in this and every generation to come. It is the obligation of all who were formed by You, God of our fathers and mothers, to thank and praise You, to acclaim and glorify You, to exalt, honor, and remember You, to bless and esteem and adore You even beyond all the songs and the praises of David, Your anointed servant, offspring of Jesse and descendant of Ruth.

May Your Name be praised forever, our Source, You who are great and holy on earth and in the heavens. God of our ancestors, song and praise befit You, psalms and music belong to You. We acknowledge Your strength and governance, Your endurance, greatness, and courage; beauty and splendor, holiness and majesty become You as we give blessings and thanks to You, now and forever.

Praised are You, God of great strength, who is praised in song, God of thanksgiving, Creator of every soul, the One who chooses songs and praises, God, the life of all worlds.

Fourth Cup of Wine

הִנְנִי מוּכָן וּמְזֻמָּן לְקַיֵּם מִצְוַת כּוֹס רְבִיעִי מֵאַרְבַּע
כּוֹסוֹת לְשֵׁם יִחוּד קֻדְשָׁא בְּרִיךְ הוּא וּשְׁכִינְתֵּיהּ עַל־יְדֵי
הַהוּא טָמִיר וְנֶעְלָם בְּשֵׁם כָּל־יִשְׂרָאֵל.

I am ready and willing to enact the precept of blessing this day over the fourth cup of wine. I do this to unite God's Presence and in the name of all of Israel.

בָּרוּךְ אַתָּה יְיָ, אֱלֹהֵינוּ מֶלֶךְ הָעוֹלָם, בּוֹרֵא פְּרִי הַגָּפֶן.

Praised are You, our God, Sovereign of the Universe, who creates the fruit of the vine.

Drink while reclining to the left.

בָּרוּךְ אַתָּה יְיָ אֱלֹהֵינוּ מֶלֶךְ הָעוֹלָם עַל הַגֶּפֶן וְעַל פְּרִי
הַגֶּפֶן. וְעַל תְּנוּבַת הַשָּׂדֶה, וְעַל אֶרֶץ חֶמְדָּה טוֹבָה
וּרְחָבָה, שֶׁרָצִיתָ וְהִנְחַלְתָּ לַאֲבוֹתֵינוּ, לֶאֱכוֹל מִפִּרְיָהּ
וְלִשְׂבֹּעַ מִטּוּבָהּ. רַחֶם נָא יְיָ אֱלֹהֵינוּ עַל יִשְׂרָאֵל עַמֶּךָ,
וְעַל יְרוּשָׁלַיִם עִירֶךָ, וְעַל צִיּוֹן מִשְׁכַּן כְּבוֹדֶךָ, וְעַל מִזְבְּחֶךָ
וְעַל הֵיכָלֶךָ. וּבְנֵה יְרוּשָׁלַיִם עִיר הַקֹּדֶשׁ בִּמְהֵרָה בְיָמֵינוּ,
וְהַעֲלֵנוּ לְתוֹכָהּ, וְשַׂמְּחֵנוּ בְּבִנְיָנָהּ וְנֹאכַל מִפִּרְיָהּ וְנִשְׂבַּע
מִטּוּבָהּ, וּנְבָרֶכְךָ עָלֶיהָ בִּקְדֻשָּׁה וּבְטָהֳרָה

Praised are You, our God, Sovereign of the Universe, for the vine and for the fruit of the vine; and for the produce of the field; and for the good and spacious land that you took pleasure in giving to our ancestors, to eat from its fruits and to be full from its goodness. Have mercy, please our God, upon Your people Israel, and upon Your entire world that You created, and upon Your altar and Your sanctuary. Rebuild Jerusalem, the holy city, speedily in our days, and gladden us in its completion. Let us eat of its fruits and take pleasure in its goodness, and afterward bless You in holiness and purity.

On Shabbat say וּרְצֵה וְהַחֲלִיצֵנוּ בְּיוֹם הַשַּׁבָּת הַזֶּה.

On Shabbat say And may you be pleased with our rest on this Shabbat day.

וְשַׂמְּחֵנוּ בְּיוֹם חַג הַמַּצּוֹת הַזֶּה. כִּי אַתָּה יְיָ טוֹב וּמֵטִיב
לַכֹּל, וְנוֹדֶה לְךָ עַל הָאָרֶץ וְעַל פְּרִי הַגָּפֶן. בָּרוּךְ אַתָּה יְיָ,
עַל הָאָרֶץ וְעַל פְּרִי הַגָּפֶן.

Gladden us on this Festival of Matzot. For You, God, are good and do good for all, and we thank You for the land and for the fruit of the vine. Praised are You, God, for the land and for the fruit of the vine.

Nirtzah ○ נִרְצָה ○ Closing

חֲסַל סִדּוּר פֶּסַח כְּהִלְכָתוֹ, כְּכָל מִשְׁפָּטוֹ וְחֻקָּתוֹ. כַּאֲשֶׁר זָכִינוּ לְסַדֵּר אוֹתוֹ, כֵּן נִזְכֶּה לַעֲשׂוֹתוֹ. זָךְ שׁוֹכֵן מְעוֹנָה, קוֹמֵם קְהַל עֲדַת מִי מָנָה. בְּקָרוֹב נַהֵל נִטְעֵי כַנָּה, פְּדוּיִם לְצִיּוֹן בְּרִנָּה.

The Seder has concluded as it should, complete in all its various laws and customs. Just as we were privileged to arrange it tonight, so may we be granted to perform it again. O Pure One, who dwells in the heights above, establish us as a countless people once again. Speedily guide Your nation Israel, as a redeemed people, to the land of Zion with song.

לְשָׁנָה הַבָּאָה בִּירוּשָׁלָיִם

Next year, in Jerusalem, the rebuilt city!

Sefirat Ha'omer ○ סְפִירַת הָעֹמֶר ○ Counting the Omer

Outside of Israel, the counting of the omer begins on the second night of Passover at the conclusion of the Seder.

בָּרוּךְ אַתָּה יְיָ אֱלֹהֵינוּ מֶלֶךְ הָעוֹלָם, אֲשֶׁר קִדְּשָׁנוּ בְּמִצְוֹתָיו וְצִוָּנוּ עַל סְפִירַת הָעֹמֶר.

Praised are You, our God, Sovereign of the Universe, who has sanctified us through the mitzvot, and instructed us to count the omer.

הַיּוֹם יוֹם אֶחָד לָעֹמֶר.

Today is one day of the omer.

hope-giver

Jerusalem—the First Among Visions

A slave has no hope.

Yesterday, today, and tomorrow are all the same for a slave. And hoping for a better life—for change—invites bitter disappointment.

In contrast, a free person dares to envision change, to imagine a better future.

At the culmination of the Seder we dare to proclaim, "Next year in Jerusalem." We have been saying this for two thousand years, through good years and bad. We are free—free to dream, free to create. It doesn't get more powerful than this.

Abraham Joshua Heschel writes, "Jerusalem is not the first among cities. She is the first among visions. Her power is in her promise. What is the mystery of Jerusalem? A promise: peace and God's presence." At the Seder, we dare to dream. And we end the Seder by envisioning utopia.

Appreciate the beauty and depth of the Seder's final moment! Get everyone up, dance around the table and sing "*L'shana Haba'a b'Yerushalayim*" at the top of your lungs!

Have everyone share a "Jerusalem moment," a high point they experienced in Jerusalem or that could only happen in Jerusalem.

79

Ki Lo Na'e ∘ כִּי לוֹ נָאֶה ∘ Mighty in Sovereignty

כִּי לוֹ נָאֶה, כִּי לוֹ יָאֶה.

For to God, it is fitting, for to God, it shall be fitting.

אַדִּיר בִּמְלוּכָה, בָּחוּר כַּהֲלָכָה, גְּדוּדָיו יֹאמְרוּ לוֹ:
לְךָ וּלְךָ, לְךָ כִּי לְךָ, לְךָ אַף לְךָ, לְךָ יְיָ הַמַּמְלָכָה.
כִּי לוֹ נָאֶה, כִּי לוֹ יָאֶה.

Mighty in sovereignty, distinguished on God's path, God's divine retinue will declare: [Refrain] to You, and for You, to You, because of You, to You, particularly to You, to You, God, belongs sovereignty. For to God, it is fitting, for to God, it shall be fitting.

דָּגוּל בִּמְלוּכָה, הָדוּר כַּהֲלָכָה, וְתִיקָיו יֹאמְרוּ לוֹ:
לְךָ וּלְךָ, לְךָ כִּי לְךָ, לְךָ אַף לְךָ, לְךָ יְיָ הַמַּמְלָכָה.
כִּי לוֹ נָאֶה, כִּי לוֹ יָאֶה.

Exalted in sovereignty, glorious on God's path, God's faithful ones will declare: [Refrain]

זַכַּאי בִּמְלוּכָה, חָסִין כַּהֲלָכָה, טַפְסְרָיו יֹאמְרוּ לוֹ:
לְךָ וּלְךָ, לְךָ כִּי לְךָ, לְךָ אַף לְךָ, לְךָ יְיָ הַמַּמְלָכָה.
כִּי לוֹ נָאֶה, כִּי לוֹ יָאֶה.

Faultless in sovereignty, kind on God's path, God's appointed ones will declare: [Refrain]

יָחִיד בִּמְלוּכָה, כַּבִּיר כַּהֲלָכָה, לִמּוּדָיו יֹאמְרוּ לוֹ:
לְךָ וּלְךָ, לְךָ כִּי לְךָ, לְךָ אַף לְךָ, לְךָ יְיָ הַמַּמְלָכָה.
כִּי לוֹ נָאֶה, כִּי לוֹ יָאֶה.

Unique in sovereignty, illustrious on God's path, God's wise ones will declare: [Refrain]

מוֹשֵׁל בִּמְלוּכָה, נוֹרָא כַּהֲלָכָה, סְבִיבָיו יֹאמְרוּ לוֹ:
לְךָ וּלְךָ, לְךָ כִּי לְךָ, לְךָ אַף לְךָ, לְךָ יְיָ הַמַּמְלָכָה.
כִּי לוֹ נָאֶה, כִּי לוֹ יָאֶה.

Supreme in sovereignty, awe-inspiring on God's path, those who surround God will declare: [Refrain]

עָנָו בִּמְלוּכָה, פּוֹדֶה כַּהֲלָכָה, צַדִּיקָיו יֹאמְרוּ לוֹ:
לְךָ וּלְךָ, לְךָ כִּי לְךָ, לְךָ אַף לְךָ, לְךָ יְיָ הַמַּמְלָכָה.
כִּי לוֹ נָאֶה, כִּי לוֹ יָאֶה.

Humble in sovereignty, honorable on God's path, God's righteous ones will declare: [Refrain]

קָדוֹשׁ בִּמְלוּכָה, רַחוּם כַּהֲלָכָה, שִׁנְאַנָּיו יֹאמְרוּ לוֹ:
לְךָ וּלְךָ, לְךָ כִּי לְךָ, לְךָ אַף לְךָ, לְךָ יְיָ הַמַּמְלָכָה.
כִּי לוֹ נָאֶה, כִּי לוֹ יָאֶה.

Holy in sovereignty, merciful on God's path, God's followers will declare: [Refrain]

תַּקִּיף בִּמְלוּכָה, תּוֹמֵךְ כַּהֲלָכָה, תְּמִימָיו יֹאמְרוּ לוֹ:
לְךָ וּלְךָ, לְךָ כִּי לְךָ, לְךָ אַף לְךָ, לְךָ יְיָ הַמַּמְלָכָה.
כִּי לוֹ נָאֶה, כִּי לוֹ יָאֶה.

Resolute in sovereignty, supportive on God's path, God's perfect ones will declare: [Refrain]

Adir Hu ∘ אַדִּיר הוּא ∘ Distinguished Is God

[Refrain] יִבְנֶה בֵיתוֹ בְּקָרוֹב, בִּמְהֵרָה בִּמְהֵרָה, בְּיָמֵינוּ בְּקָרוֹב. אֵל בְּנֵה, בְּנֵה בֵיתְךָ בְּקָרוֹב.

[Refrain] Mighty is God. May God build God's dwelling place speedily, in our days. God, rebuild Your dwelling place!

אַדִּיר הוּא, יִבְנֶה בֵיתוֹ בְּקָרוֹב, בִּמְהֵרָה בִּמְהֵרָה, בְּיָמֵינוּ בְּקָרוֹב. אֵל בְּנֵה, בְּנֵה בֵיתְךָ בְּקָרוֹב.

Distinguished is God, great is God, exalted is God. [Refrain]

בָּחוּר הוּא, גָּדוֹל הוּא, דָּגוּל הוּא, יִבְנֶה בֵיתוֹ בְּקָרוֹב, בִּמְהֵרָה בִּמְהֵרָה, בְּיָמֵינוּ בְּקָרוֹב. אֵל בְּנֵה, אֵל בְּנֵה, בְּנֵה בֵיתְךָ בְּקָרוֹב.

Glorious is God, faithful is God, faultless is God. [Refrain]

הָדוּר הוּא, וָתִיק הוּא, זַכַּאי הוּא, חָסִיד הוּא, יִבְנֶה בֵיתוֹ בְּקָרוֹב, בִּמְהֵרָה בִּמְהֵרָה, בְּיָמֵינוּ בְּקָרוֹב. אֵל בְּנֵה, אֵל בְּנֵה, בְּנֵה בֵיתְךָ בְּקָרוֹב.

Powerful is God, wise is God, sovereign is God. [Refrain]

טָהוֹר הוּא, יָחִיד הוּא, כַּבִּיר הוּא, יִבְנֶה בֵיתוֹ בְּקָרוֹב, בִּמְהֵרָה בִּמְהֵרָה, בְּיָמֵינוּ בְּקָרוֹב. אֵל בְּנֵה, אֵל בְּנֵה, בְּנֵה בֵיתְךָ בְּקָרוֹב.

Illuminating is God, sublime is God, powerful is God. [Refrain]

לָמוּד הוּא, מֶלֶךְ הוּא, נוֹרָא הוּא, יִבְנֶה בֵיתוֹ בְּקָרוֹב, בִּמְהֵרָה בִּמְהֵרָה, בְּיָמֵינוּ בְּקָרוֹב. אֵל בְּנֵה, אֵל בְּנֵה, בְּנֵה בֵיתְךָ בְּקָרוֹב.

Honorable is God, righteous is God, holy is God. [Refrain]

סַגִּיב הוּא, עִזּוּז הוּא, פּוֹדֶה הוּא, צַדִּיק הוּא, יִבְנֶה בֵיתוֹ בְּקָרוֹב, בִּמְהֵרָה בִּמְהֵרָה, בְּיָמֵינוּ בְּקָרוֹב. אֵל בְּנֵה, אֵל בְּנֵה, בְּנֵה בֵיתְךָ בְּקָרוֹב.

Exalted is God, strong is God, redeemer is God, righteous is God. [Refrain]

קָדוֹשׁ הוּא, רַחוּם הוּא, שַׁדַּי הוּא, תַּקִּיף הוּא, יִבְנֶה בֵיתוֹ בְּקָרוֹב, בִּמְהֵרָה בִּמְהֵרָה, בְּיָמֵינוּ בְּקָרוֹב. אֵל בְּנֵה, אֵל בְּנֵה, בְּנֵה בֵיתְךָ בְּקָרוֹב.

Merciful is God, almighty is God, preeminent is God. [Refrain]

Echad Mi Yodea • אֶחָד מִי יוֹדֵעַ • Who Knows One

1 אֶחָד מִי יוֹדֵעַ? אֶחָד אֲנִי יוֹדֵעַ: אֶחָד אֱלֹהֵינוּ שֶׁבַּשָּׁמַיִם וּבָאָרֶץ.

Who knows one? I know one:
One is our God, in heaven and earth.

2 שְׁנַיִם מִי יוֹדֵעַ? שְׁנַיִם אֲנִי יוֹדֵעַ: שְׁנֵי לֻחוֹת הַבְּרִית,
אֶחָד אֱלֹהֵינוּ שֶׁבַּשָּׁמַיִם וּבָאָרֶץ.

Who knows two? I know two:
Two are the Tablets of the Covenant.
One is our God, in heaven and earth.

3 שְׁלֹשָׁה מִי יוֹדֵעַ? שְׁלֹשָׁה אֲנִי יוֹדֵעַ: שְׁלֹשָׁה אָבוֹת, שְׁנֵי לֻחוֹת הַבְּרִית,
אֶחָד אֱלֹהֵינוּ שֶׁבַּשָּׁמַיִם וּבָאָרֶץ.

Who knows three? I know three:
Three are the patriarchs.

4 אַרְבַּע מִי יוֹדֵעַ? אַרְבַּע אֲנִי יוֹדֵעַ: אַרְבַּע אִמָּהוֹת, שְׁלֹשָׁה אָבוֹת,
שְׁנֵי לֻחוֹת הַבְּרִית, אֶחָד אֱלֹהֵינוּ שֶׁבַּשָּׁמַיִם וּבָאָרֶץ.

Who knows four? I know four:
Four are the matriarchs.

5 חֲמִשָּׁה מִי יוֹדֵעַ? חֲמִשָּׁה אֲנִי יוֹדֵעַ: חֲמִשָּׁה חֻמְשֵׁי תוֹרָה, אַרְבַּע אִמָּהוֹת,
שְׁלֹשָׁה אָבוֹת, שְׁנֵי לֻחוֹת הַבְּרִית, אֶחָד אֱלֹהֵינוּ שֶׁבַּשָּׁמַיִם וּבָאָרֶץ.

Who knows five? I know five:
Five are the books of Torah.

6 שִׁשָּׁה מִי יוֹדֵעַ? שִׁשָּׁה אֲנִי יוֹדֵעַ: שִׁשָּׁה סִדְרֵי מִשְׁנָה, חֲמִשָּׁה חֻמְשֵׁי תוֹרָה,
אַרְבַּע אִמָּהוֹת, שְׁלֹשָׁה אָבוֹת, שְׁנֵי לֻחוֹת הַבְּרִית, אֶחָד אֱלֹהֵינוּ שֶׁבַּשָּׁמַיִם וּבָאָרֶץ.

Who knows six? I know six:
Six are the orders of Mishnah.

7 שִׁבְעָה מִי יוֹדֵעַ? שִׁבְעָה אֲנִי יוֹדֵעַ: שִׁבְעָה יְמֵי שַׁבַּתָּא, שִׁשָּׁה סִדְרֵי מִשְׁנָה,
חֲמִשָּׁה חֻמְשֵׁי תוֹרָה, אַרְבַּע אִמָּהוֹת, שְׁלֹשָׁה אָבוֹת, שְׁנֵי לֻחוֹת הַבְּרִית,
אֶחָד אֱלֹהֵינוּ שֶׁבַּשָּׁמַיִם וּבָאָרֶץ.

Who knows seven? I know seven:
Seven are the days of the week.

8 שְׁמוֹנָה מִי יוֹדֵעַ? שְׁמוֹנָה אֲנִי יוֹדֵעַ: שְׁמוֹנָה יְמֵי מִילָה, שִׁבְעָה יְמֵי שַׁבַּתָּא,
שִׁשָּׁה סִדְרֵי מִשְׁנָה, חֲמִשָּׁה חֻמְשֵׁי תוֹרָה, אַרְבַּע אִמָּהוֹת, שְׁלֹשָׁה אָבוֹת,
שְׁנֵי לֻחוֹת הַבְּרִית, אֶחָד אֱלֹהֵינוּ שֶׁבַּשָּׁמַיִם וּבָאָרֶץ.

Who knows eight? I know eight:
Eight are the days before a *b'rit milah*.

82

9 Who knows nine? I know nine:
Nine are the months of pregnancy.

תִּשְׁעָה מִי יוֹדֵעַ? תִּשְׁעָה אֲנִי יוֹדֵעַ: תִּשְׁעָה יַרְחֵי לֵדָה, שְׁמוֹנָה יְמֵי מִילָה, שִׁבְעָה יְמֵי שַׁבַּתָּא, שִׁשָּׁה סִדְרֵי מִשְׁנָה, חֲמִשָּׁה חֻמְשֵׁי תוֹרָה, אַרְבַּע אִמָּהוֹת, שְׁלֹשָׁה אָבוֹת, שְׁנֵי לֻחוֹת הַבְּרִית, אֶחָד אֱלֹהֵינוּ שֶׁבַּשָּׁמַיִם וּבָאָרֶץ.

10 Who knows ten? I know ten:
Ten are the commandments.

עֲשָׂרָה מִי יוֹדֵעַ? עֲשָׂרָה אֲנִי יוֹדֵעַ: עֲשָׂרָה דִבְּרַיָא, תִּשְׁעָה יַרְחֵי לֵדָה, שְׁמוֹנָה יְמֵי מִילָה, שִׁבְעָה יְמֵי שַׁבַּתָּא, שִׁשָּׁה סִדְרֵי מִשְׁנָה, חֲמִשָּׁה חֻמְשֵׁי תוֹרָה, אַרְבַּע אִמָּהוֹת, שְׁלֹשָׁה אָבוֹת, שְׁנֵי לֻחוֹת הַבְּרִית, אֶחָד אֱלֹהֵינוּ שֶׁבַּשָּׁמַיִם וּבָאָרֶץ.

11 Who knows eleven? I know eleven:
Eleven are the stars in Joseph's dream.

אַחַד עָשָׂר מִי יוֹדֵעַ? אַחַד עָשָׂר אֲנִי יוֹדֵעַ: אַחַד עָשָׂר כּוֹכְבַיָא, עֲשָׂרָה דִבְּרַיָא, תִּשְׁעָה יַרְחֵי לֵדָה, שְׁמוֹנָה יְמֵי מִילָה, שִׁבְעָה יְמֵי שַׁבַּתָּא, שִׁשָּׁה סִדְרֵי מִשְׁנָה, חֲמִשָּׁה חֻמְשֵׁי תוֹרָה, אַרְבַּע אִמָּהוֹת, שְׁלֹשָׁה אָבוֹת, שְׁנֵי לֻחוֹת הַבְּרִית, אֶחָד אֱלֹהֵינוּ שֶׁבַּשָּׁמַיִם וּבָאָרֶץ.

12 Who knows twelve? I know twelve:
Twelve are the tribes of Israel.

שְׁנֵים עָשָׂר מִי יוֹדֵעַ? שְׁנֵים עָשָׂר אֲנִי יוֹדֵעַ: שְׁנֵים עָשָׂר שִׁבְטַיָא, אַחַד עָשָׂר כּוֹכְבַיָא, עֲשָׂרָה דִבְּרַיָא, תִּשְׁעָה יַרְחֵי לֵדָה, שְׁמוֹנָה יְמֵי מִילָה, שִׁבְעָה יְמֵי שַׁבַּתָּא, שִׁשָּׁה סִדְרֵי מִשְׁנָה, חֲמִשָּׁה חֻמְשֵׁי תוֹרָה, אַרְבַּע אִמָּהוֹת, שְׁלֹשָׁה אָבוֹת, שְׁנֵי לֻחוֹת הַבְּרִית, אֶחָד אֱלֹהֵינוּ שֶׁבַּשָּׁמַיִם וּבָאָרֶץ.

13 Who knows thirteen? I know thirteen:
Thirteen are the attributes of God.

שְׁלֹשָׁה עָשָׂר מִי יוֹדֵעַ? שְׁלֹשָׁה עָשָׂר אֲנִי יוֹדֵעַ: שְׁלֹשָׁה עָשָׂר מִדַּיָא, שְׁנֵים עָשָׂר שִׁבְטַיָא, אַחַד עָשָׂר כּוֹכְבַיָא, עֲשָׂרָה דִבְּרַיָא, תִּשְׁעָה יַרְחֵי לֵדָה, שְׁמוֹנָה יְמֵי מִילָה, שִׁבְעָה יְמֵי שַׁבַּתָּא, שִׁשָּׁה סִדְרֵי מִשְׁנָה, חֲמִשָּׁה חֻמְשֵׁי תוֹרָה, אַרְבַּע אִמָּהוֹת, שְׁלֹשָׁה אָבוֹת, שְׁנֵי לֻחוֹת הַבְּרִית, אֶחָד אֱלֹהֵינוּ שֶׁבַּשָּׁמַיִם וּבָאָרֶץ.

Chad Gad'ya ◦ חַד גַּדְיָא ◦ One Little Kid

חַד גַּדְיָא, חַד גַּדְיָא

One little kid, one little kid

דְּזַבִּין אַבָּא בִּתְרֵי זוּזֵי, חַד גַּדְיָא, חַד גַּדְיָא.

One little kid,
that my father bought for two *zuzim*, *chad gad'ya*.

וְאָתָא שׁוּנְרָא, וְאָכְלָה לְגַדְיָא,
דְּזַבִּין אַבָּא בִּתְרֵי זוּזֵי, חַד גַּדְיָא, חַד גַּדְיָא.

Then came a cat, that ate the kid,
that my father bought for two *zuzim*, *chad gad'ya*.

וְאָתָא כַלְבָּא, וְנָשַׁךְ לְשׁוּנְרָא, דְּאָכְלָה לְגַדְיָא,
דְּזַבִּין אַבָּא בִּתְרֵי זוּזֵי, חַד גַּדְיָא, חַד גַּדְיָא.

Then came a dog, that bit the cat, that ate the kid, that my
father bought for two *zuzim*, *chad gad'ya*.

וְאָתָא חוּטְרָא, וְהִכָּה לְכַלְבָּא, דְּנָשַׁךְ לְשׁוּנְרָא, דְּאָכְלָה לְגַדְיָא,
דְּזַבִּין אַבָּא בִּתְרֵי זוּזֵי, חַד גַּדְיָא, חַד גַּדְיָא.

Then came a stick, that beat the dog, that bit the cat, that ate
the kid, that my father bought for two *zuzim*, *chad gad'ya*.

וְאָתָא נוּרָא, וְשָׂרַף לְחוּטְרָא, דְּהִכָּה לְכַלְבָּא, דְּנָשַׁךְ לְשׁוּנְרָא,
דְּאָכְלָה לְגַדְיָא, דְּזַבִּין אַבָּא בִּתְרֵי זוּזֵי, חַד גַּדְיָא, חַד גַּדְיָא.

Then came a fire, that burnt the stick, that beat the dog, that
bit the cat, that ate the kid, that my father bought for two
zuzim, *chad gad'ya*.

וְאָתָא מַיָּא, וְכָבָה לְנוּרָא, דְּשָׂרַף לְחוּטְרָא, דְּהִכָּה לְכַלְבָּא,
דְּנָשַׁךְ לְשׁוּנְרָא, דְּאָכְלָה לְגַדְיָא,
דְּזַבִּין אַבָּא בִּתְרֵי זוּזֵי, חַד גַּדְיָא, חַד גַּדְיָא.

Then came a water, that quenched the fire, that burnt the
stick, that beat the dog, that bit the cat, that my father bought
for two *zuzim*, *chad gad'ya*.

וְאָתָא תוֹרָא, וְשָׁתָא לְמַיָּא, דְּכָבָה לְנוּרָא, דְּשָׂרַף לְחוּטְרָא,
דְּהִכָּה לְכַלְבָּא, דְּנָשַׁךְ לְשׁוּנְרָא, דְּאָכְלָה לְגַדְיָא,
דְּזַבִּין אַבָּא בִּתְרֵי זוּזֵי, חַד גַּדְיָא, חַד גַּדְיָא.

Then came an ox, that drank the water, that quenched the
fire, that burnt the stick, that beat the dog, that bit the cat,
that ate the kid, that my father bought for two *zuzim*, *chad
gad'ya*.

וְאָתָא הַשּׁוֹחֵט, וְשָׁחַט לְתוֹרָא, דְּשָׁתָא לְמַיָּא,
דְּכָבָה לְנוּרָא, דְּשָׂרַף לְחוּטְרָא, דְּהִכָּה לְכַלְבָּא,
דְּנָשַׁךְ לְשׁוּנְרָא, דְּאָכְלָה לְגַדְיָא,
דְּזַבִּין אַבָּא בִּתְרֵי זוּזֵי, חַד גַּדְיָא, חַד גַּדְיָא.

Then came a slaughterer, who slaughtered the ox,
that drank the water, that quenched the fire,
that burnt the stick, that beat the dog, that bit the cat,
that ate the kid, that my father bought for two *zuzim, chad gad'ya.*

וְאָתָא מַלְאַךְ הַמָּוֶת, וְשָׁחַט לְשׁוֹחֵט, דְּשָׁחַט לְתוֹרָא,
דְּשָׁתָא לְמַיָּא, דְּכָבָה לְנוּרָא, דְּשָׂרַף לְחוּטְרָא,
דְּהִכָּה לְכַלְבָּא, דְּנָשַׁךְ לְשׁוּנְרָא, דְּאָכְלָה לְגַדְיָא,
דְּזַבִּין אַבָּא בִּתְרֵי זוּזֵי, חַד גַּדְיָא, חַד גַּדְיָא.

Then came the Angel of Death, who slew the slaughterer,
who slaughtered the ox, that drank the water,
that quenched the fire, that burnt the stick, that beat the dog,
that bit the cat, that ate the kid,
that my father bought for two *zuzim, chad gad'ya.*

וְאָתָא הַקָּדוֹשׁ בָּרוּךְ הוּא,

Then came the Holy One, who slew the Angel of Death,

וְשָׁחַט לְמַלְאַךְ הַמָּוֶת,

who slew the slaughterer,

דְּשָׁחַט לְתוֹרָא,

who slaughtered the ox,

דְּשָׁתָא לְמַיָּא,

that drank the water,

דְּכָבָה לְנוּרָא,

that quenched the fire,

דְּשָׂרַף לְחוּטְרָא,

that burnt the stick,

דְּהִכָּה לְכַלְבָּא,

that beat the dog,

דְּנָשַׁךְ לְשׁוּנְרָא,

that bit the cat,

דְּאָכְלָה לְגַדְיָא,

that ate the kid,

דְּזַבִּין אַבָּא בִּתְרֵי זוּזֵי, חַד גַּדְיָא, חַד גַּדְיָא.

that my father bought for two *zuzim, chad gad'ya.*

אַיֶּכָּה Ayeka   The *Ayeka* Story

Aryeh Ben David was born in the United States and moved to Israel in 1978. He received rabbinical ordination from the Israeli Rabbinate. He was senior staff and director of spiritual education at the Pardes Institute in Jerusalem from 1987 to 2003. From 2003 to 2006 he served as the rabbinical educational consultant for Hillel International. He is the author of *Around the Shabbat Table: A Guide to Fulfilling and Meaningful Shabbat Table Conversations*, *The Godfile: 10 Approaches to Personalizing Prayer*, and *Becoming a Soulful Educator*.

In 2006, he founded *Ayeka*: Center for Soulful Education, which affirms that the goal of learning Jewish wisdom is to affect and evoke our better selves. To do this, we need to recognize that the mind learns differently than the heart, learning needs to engage our souls, and the ultimate goal of acquiring Jewish knowledge is to impact our everyday lives.

Ayeka developed a unique innovative educational approach that enables us to bring Jewish wisdom from our minds, to our hearts, to our souls, and into our lives, while honoring that every individual is on his or her own unique path, at his or her unique pace. We are all works-in-progress and Jewish wisdom is the key to our becoming our better selves.

Ayeka ("Where are you?) was created to provide this opportunity. *Ayeka*'s program tracks include:

- Becoming a Soulful Human Being
- Becoming a Soulful Family
- Becoming a Soulful Educator
- Becoming a Soulful Organization

Participants include rabbis, educators, Jewish professionals, parents, grandparents, and individual learners from every denomination who want *more*; who want a method of engaging with traditional Jewish wisdom that enables them to clarify their own unique paths and purpose, that impacts and enhances their lives.

Yoram Raanan

Yoram Raanan graduated from the University of Arts, Philadelphia. He settled in Israel in 1977.

Raanan's paintings are a modern expression of Jewish collective consciousness. Characterized by intuition and imagination, his art conveys a strong sense of light, color, and spirituality. He is inspired by the Bible, nature, and the Land of Israel.

"My work expresses something inexplicable—feeling, sensation, emotion, and spirituality. The various levels and layers of paint correspond to different possible interpretations of the work. I want to share the sense of discovery that I feel, the dynamic passion, energy flow, and color vibration, to connect the viewer with a greater sense of self and place in the world.

On the night of November 25, 2016, another chapter in our journey of faith began as a fire swept through our moshav, destroying the Raanan studio, burning hundreds and hundreds of paintings. From the first moment of watching the studio go up in flames, the absolute belief that this was God's plan was kindled from a place of trust that everything is for a higher good, as well as the hope that this be the beginning of something greater. We continue to make the journey from darkness to hope over and over since the first Exodus." For more about the artist, visit: www.yoramraanan.com.

Acknowledgments

The writing, editing, designing, and publishing of this haggadah was accompanied by many angels.

From beginning to end, the Ayeka staff—Yehoshua Looks, Tal Attia, and Dasee Berkowitz—shaped this project. The insights of Ayeka board members, David Kahn and Clare Goldwater, are felt on every page. Noga Fisher's impeccable writing and editing enriched the commentary.

The covers and aesthetic beauty of this haggadah are the blessing of our creative designers Jen Klor and Ayeka's Leora Niderberg. They, along with Emily Wichland, our publishing consultant, shepherded this haggadah with consummate grace, kindness, wisdom, and compassion. We would have been lost without you.

Yoram Raanan is this generation's soulful artist, whose personal story of journey and hope resonates with the message of this haggadah. We are honored to have one of his works grace our cover. Noam Zion graciously shared his haggadah publishing wisdom and experience.

To all of you, the countless meaningful seders emerging from this haggadah will be a tribute to your efforts.

87

Writing Page